Simon and Garfunkel's Greatest Hits
Guitar (with tablature)

Distributed by Music Sales Limited,14/15 Berners Street, London W1T 2LJ, UK.

Foreword

In order to clarify notation, Tablature has been used. For those unfamiliar with this form of notation, it is a graphic way of showing which notes are played on the guitar and where they are played.

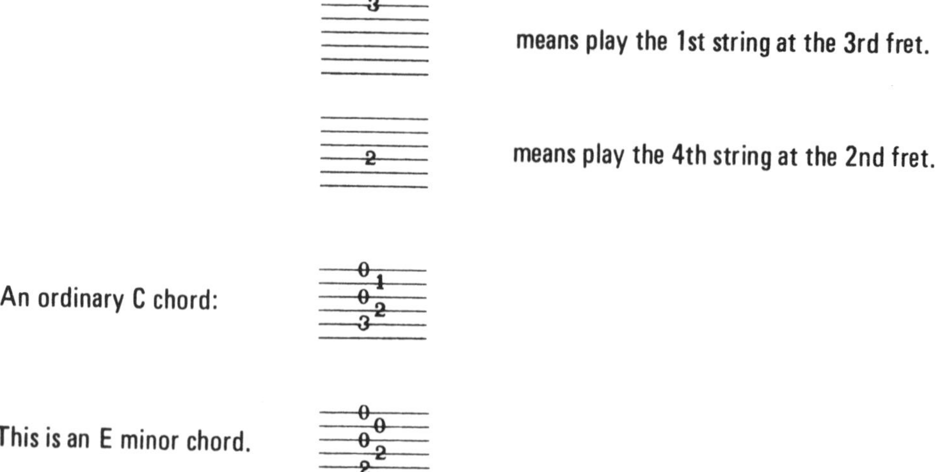

Other notation used:

1. The right hand fingers (written below the Tablature when necessary) T = thumb; I = index finger; M = middle finger;
2. R = ring finger.
3. The slur means 0 ⌒ 2 (H) hammer on; 2 ⌒ 0 (PO) pull off
4. The arpeggio (⌇) means play the notes in the chord rapidly from lower to higher (literally: in the style of a harp).
5. Brush strokes are indicated by arrows:

   ↑ means from lower strings to higher:

   ↓ vice versa
6. Rhythms of the various figures are notated below the Tab. in cue size: or by adding stems to the numbers.
7. ⁒ means, repeat the previous measure exactly.
8. ⁒⁒ means, repeat the previous two measures exactly
9. Rhythm chords are generally the ordinary open string forms familiar to every guitarist.

Mrs. Robinson

For recorded key, Capo up 2 frets

Words and Music by
PAUL SIMON

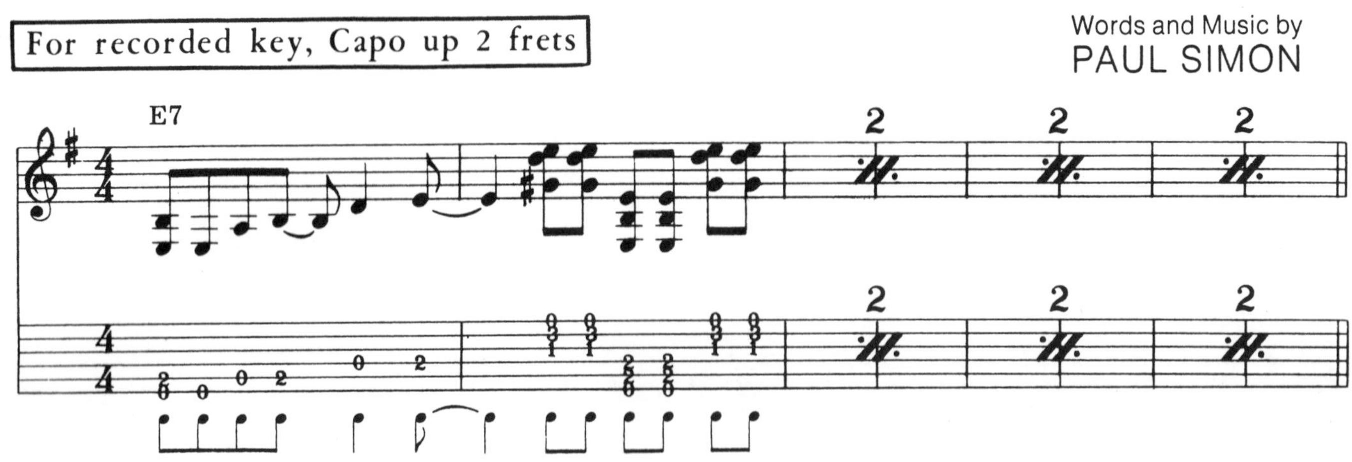

Verse:

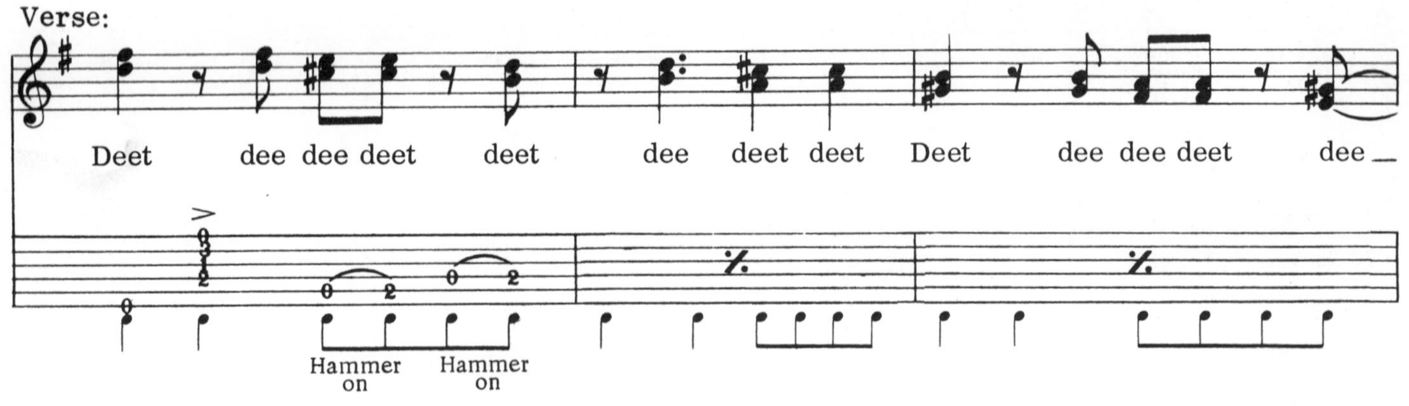

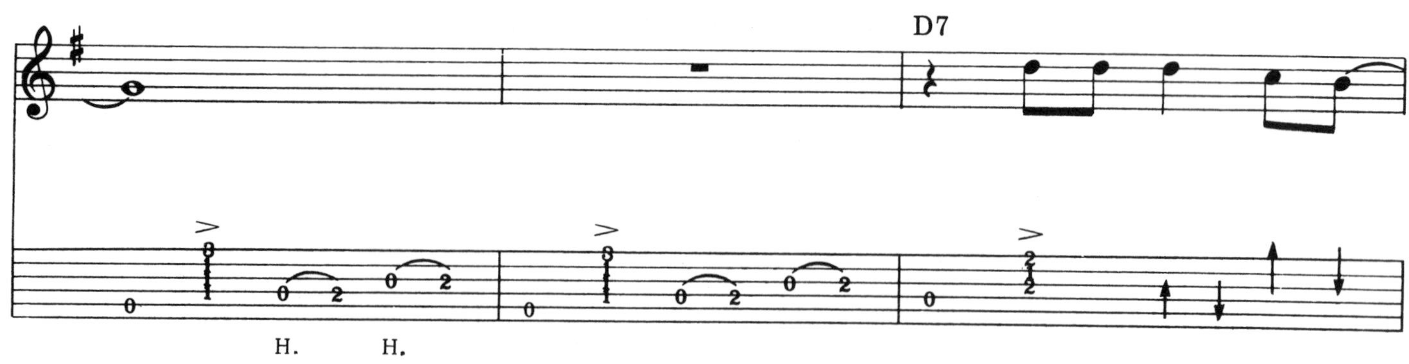
D7
H. H.

G
C
Am

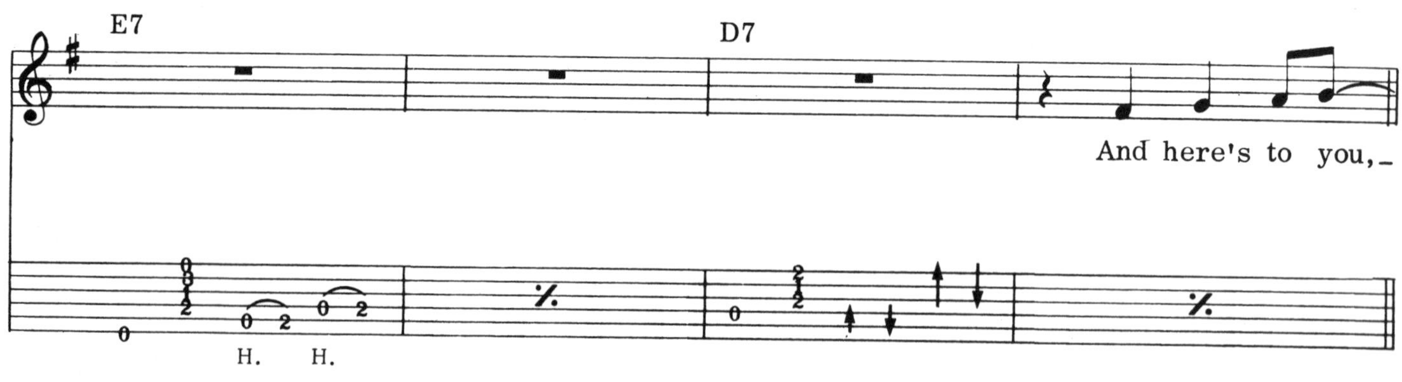
E7
D7
And here's to you,
H. H.

Chorus:

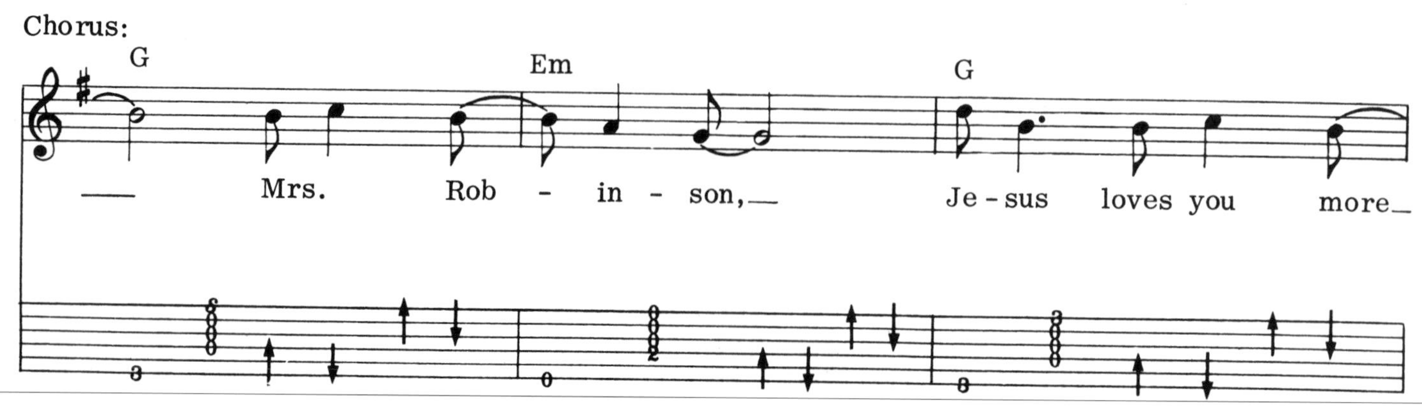
G
Em
G
Mrs. Rob - in - son,
Je - sus loves you more

Other verses and choruses continue as above. [See next page]

Additional Words

```
              E7  /   /   / / /  /   / /    /   /   /  /  / / /  / / /
Verse :We'd like to know a little bit about you for our files
         /  A7  /  /   /    /    /  /   /   / / / /  / / / /
        We'd like to help you learn to help yourself.
      D7   /     /    /     G   /   /   /    C   /   / / Am / / /  / / / /
        Look around you, all you see are sympathetic eyes
       E  / / / /  /   /   /      / D7 /   /   /   /
        Stroll around the grounds until you feel at home.
         /   /    / G  / / /  Em  /  /  /
Chorus : And here's to you, Mrs. Robinson,
        G  /  /   /   Em   /   /   /   C  /  C/B  /  C/A  /
        Jesus loves you more than you will know
        C/G  /  D/  D/C  /  D/B
        Wo, wo wo
         /  D/A  /  G  /   / /  Em / / /
        God bless you, please, Mrs. Robinson
        G  /  /  /  Em  /  /   /  C /  C/B  /  C/A  /
        Heaven holds a place for those who pray,
         C/G  /  Am/ / / / /  /  /  E7/ / /  / / / /  / / / /  / / / /
        Hey, hey, hey,         hey, hey, hey.
    E7  /    / / / /  /   /    /  /  / /  / / / /  / / / /
Verse:  Hide it in a hiding place where no one ever goes,
    A7  /   /   /   /  /  /  /   /   /   / / /  / / / /
        Put it in your pantry with your cupcakes,
    D7 ·  /    / / G  /   /  /  C  / /   /Am/ / /  / / / /
        It's a little secret, just the Robinson's affair,
     E  / / /  /   /     /   /  D7  /  /   /   /
        Most of all you've got to hide it from the kids.
         /   /   /  G /  /  /  Em/  /  /
Chorus: Coo, coo, cachoo, Mrs. Robinson,
        G  /   /   /   Em   /   /   / C  /  C/B /  C/A /
        Jesus loves you more than you will know,
        C/G  /   D /  D/C  /  D/B
        Wo, wo, wo
        /  D/A  /  G  /   / /  Em  /  /  /
        God bless you please, Mrs. Robinson
        G  /  /  /  Em   /   /   /  C /  C/B /  C/A /
        Heaven holds a place for those who pray,
        C/G  /   Am/ / / / /  /  /  E7 / / /  / / / /  / / / /  / / / /
        Hey, hey, hey          hey, hey, hey.
    E7  /   / / / / / / /  /  /  / / / / / /  / / / /
Verse:  Sitting on a sofa on a Sunday afternoon,
    A7  /   /   /   /   /  /  /   / / / /  / / / /
        Going to the candidates' debate,
    D7   /    /   /   /   / /  /  C    /    /  /  Am  / / /  / / / /
        Laugh about it, shout about it, When you've got to choose
     E  /    /   /   /   /  / / /   D7  / / /  /
        Ev'ry way you look at it you lose.
         /    /   /  G  /   /   /  Em  /  /
Chorus: Where have you gone, Joe DiMaggio?
        / G  /   /    /  Em  /  /   / C /  C/B / C/A / C/G  /    D /  D/C  /  D/B
        A nation turns its lonely eyes to you,             woo, woo, woo.
          /   D/A  /  G  /  /  /  Em/  /  /
        What's that you say, Mrs. Robinson,
        G  /   /   /  Em  /   /   / C/  C/B  /  C/A  /
        Joltin' Joe has left and gone away
        C/G  /   Am/ / / / /  /  /   E7/ / /  / / / /  / / / /  / / / /
        Hey, hey, hey          hey, hey, hey.
```

(Repeat from the beginning of the song and fade)

For Emily, Whenever I May Find Her

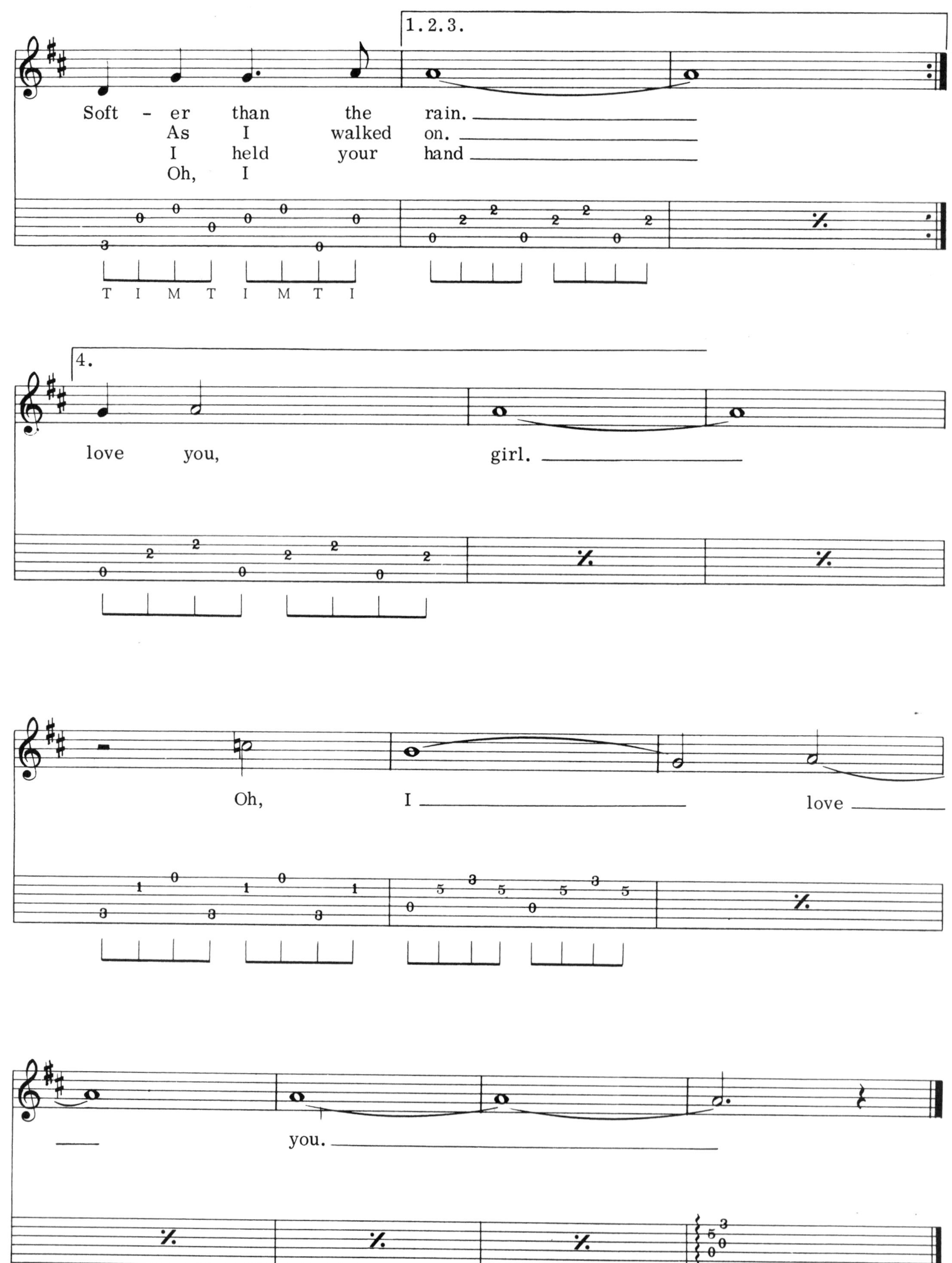
1.2.3.
Soft - er than the rain.
As I walked on.
I held your hand
Oh, I
T I M T I M T I
4.
love you, girl.
Oh, I love
you.

The Boxer

No Capo required

Words and Music by
PAUL SIMON

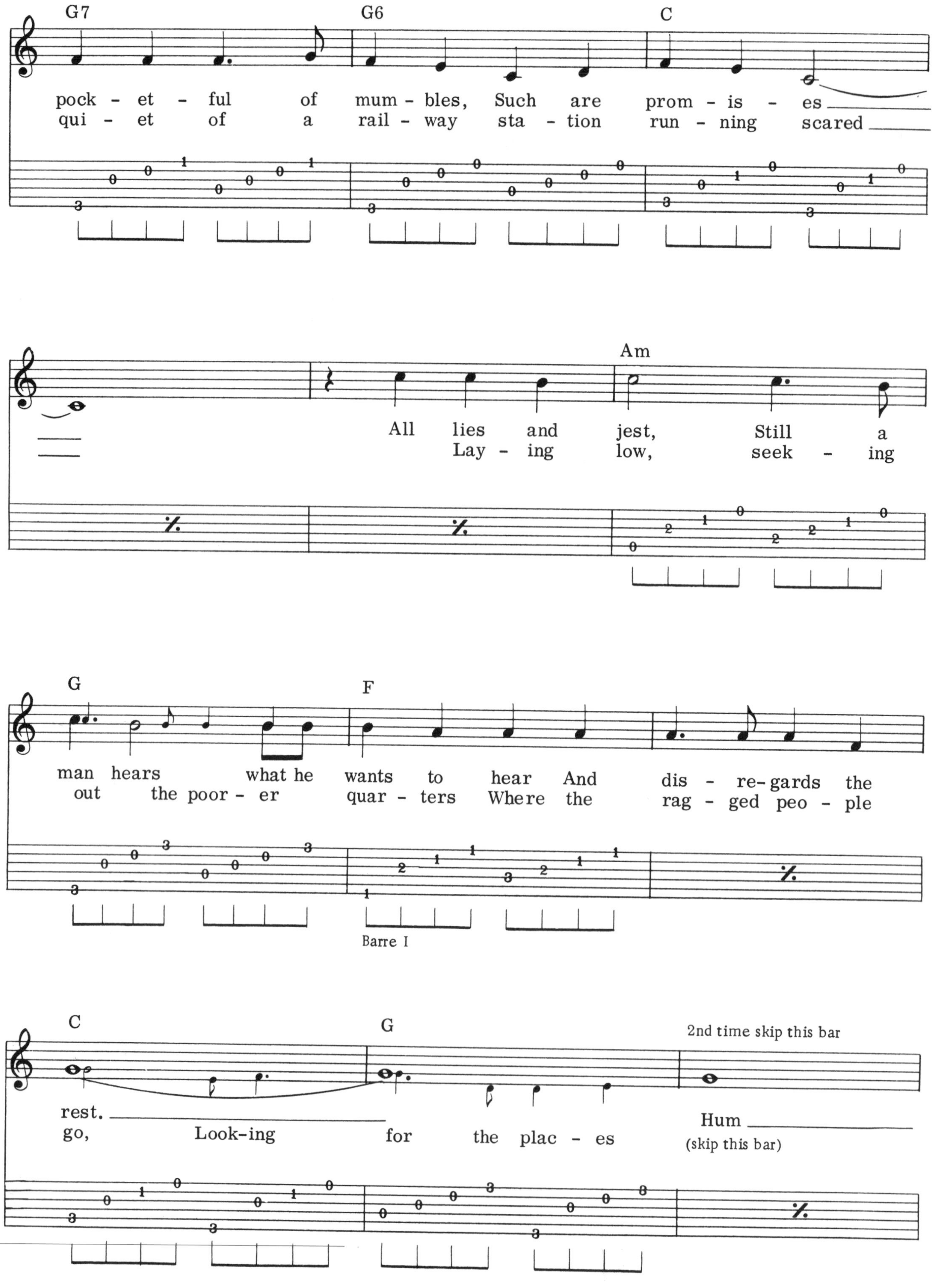

G7 G6 C

pock - et - ful of mum - bles, Such are prom - is - es
qui - et of a rail - way sta - tion run - ning scared

Am

All lies and jest, Still a
Lay - ing low, seek - ing

G F

man hears what he wants to hear And dis - re- gards the
out the poor - er quar - ters Where the rag - ged peo - ple

Barre I

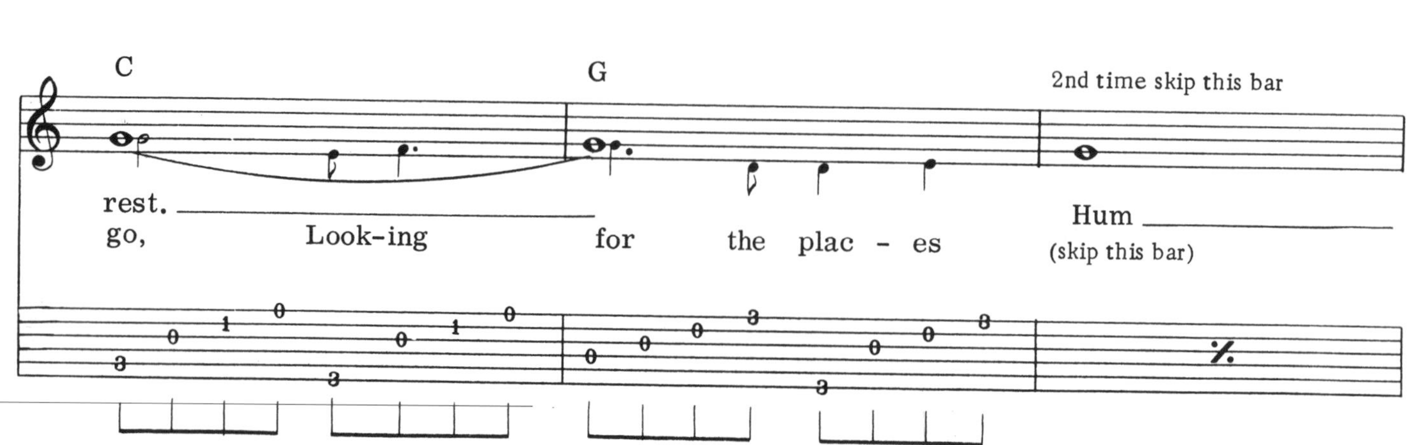

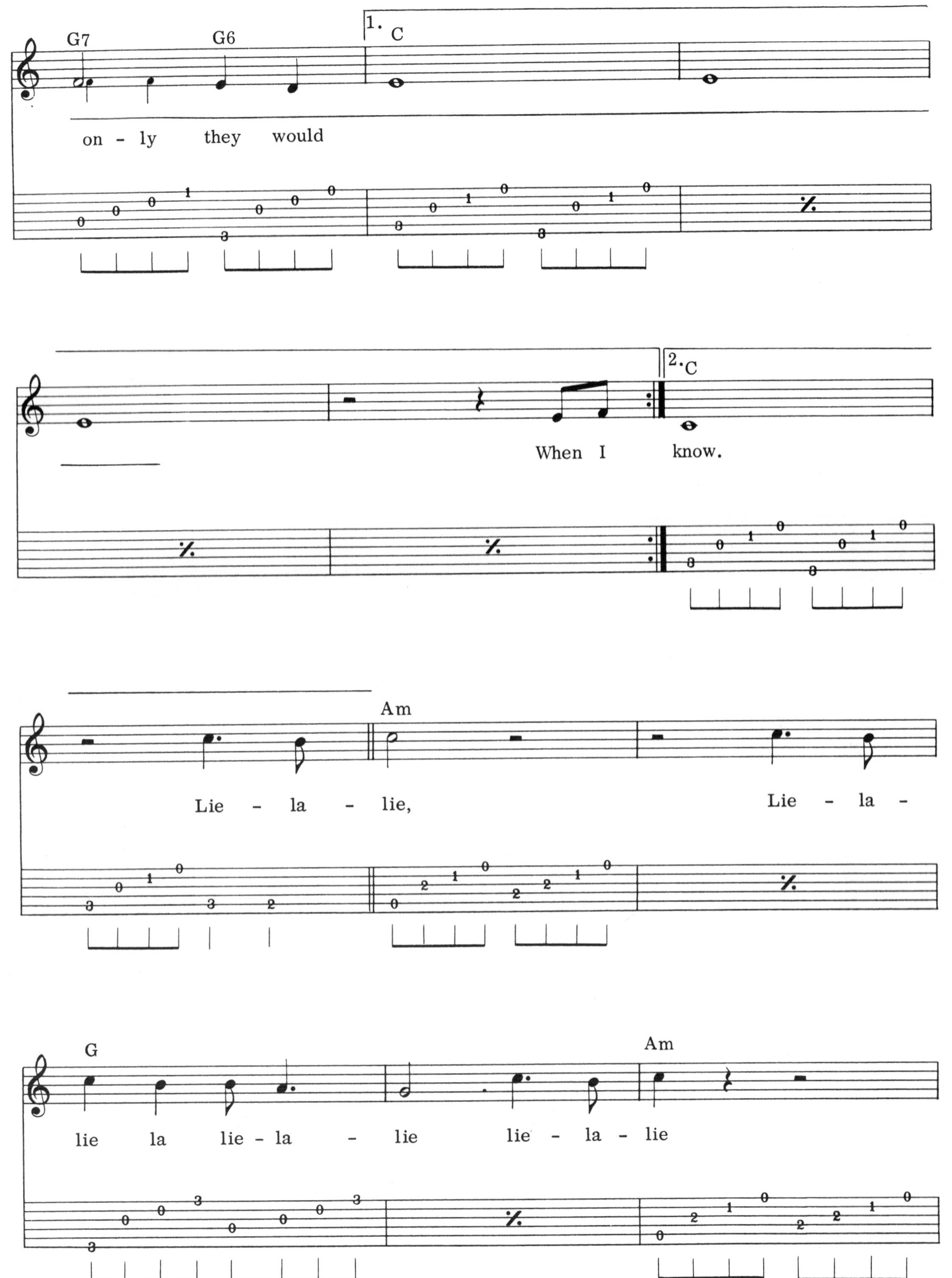
G7
G6
1.
C
on - ly
they
would
2.
C
When I
know.
Am
Lie - la - lie,
Lie - la -
G
Am
lie la
lie - la
- lie
lie - la - lie

Additional Words

Asking only workman's wages I come looking for a job
But I get no offers,
Just a come-on from the whores on Seventh Avenue
I do declare, there were times when I was so lonesome
I took some comfort there.
Ooo-la-la la la la la.

Then I'm laying out my winter clothes and wishing I was gone
Going home where the New York City winters aren't bleeding me,
Leading me, going home.

In the clearing stands a boxer and a figher by his trade
And he carries the reminders of ev'ry glove that laid him down
Or cut him till he cried out in his anger and his shame
"I am leaving, I am leaving."
But the fighter still remains.

Lie-la-la, etc.

The 59th Street Bridge Song
(FEELIN' GROOVY)

For recorded key, Capo up 3 frets

Words and Music by
PAUL SIMON

Am7 G C G/B Am7 G
Hel - lo lamp - post, what - cha know - in'
C G/B Am7 G C G/B
I've come to watch your flow - ers grow - in'. Ain't-cha got no rhymes
Am7 G C G/B Am7 G
for me? Doot - in' doo - doo, feel - in' groov - y.
C G/B Am7 G C G/B
Da da da da da da da,
Am7 G C G/B Am7 G
feel - in' groov - y. Got

C
G/B
Am7
G
no deeds to do, no prom-is - es to keep. I'm dap-pled and drow-sy and
read - y to sleep. Let the morn-ing time drop all its pet -als on me.
Life, I love you, All is groov - y.
Repeat and fade
(Hum)

The Sound of Silence

Am
Verses 2 and 3
G
si - lence.
In rest-less dreams I walked a - lone
And in the nak - ed light I saw
2 0 0 0 1 0 0 0
Brush with open hand using chords above.
Am
C
nar-row streets of cob - ble-stone,
Ten thou-sand peo - ple may-be more.
'neath the ha - lo of a
Peo - ple talk-ing with-out
F C
F C
street lamp,
speak - ing,
I turned my col-lar to the cold and damp
peo - ple hearing without lis - ten-ing
When my
Peo - ple
F
C
eyes were stabbed by the flash of a ne - on light
writ - ing songs that voic - es nev - er share
That split the
and no one
Am C G Am
night
dare
and touched the sound of si-lence.
dis- turb the sound of si-lence.

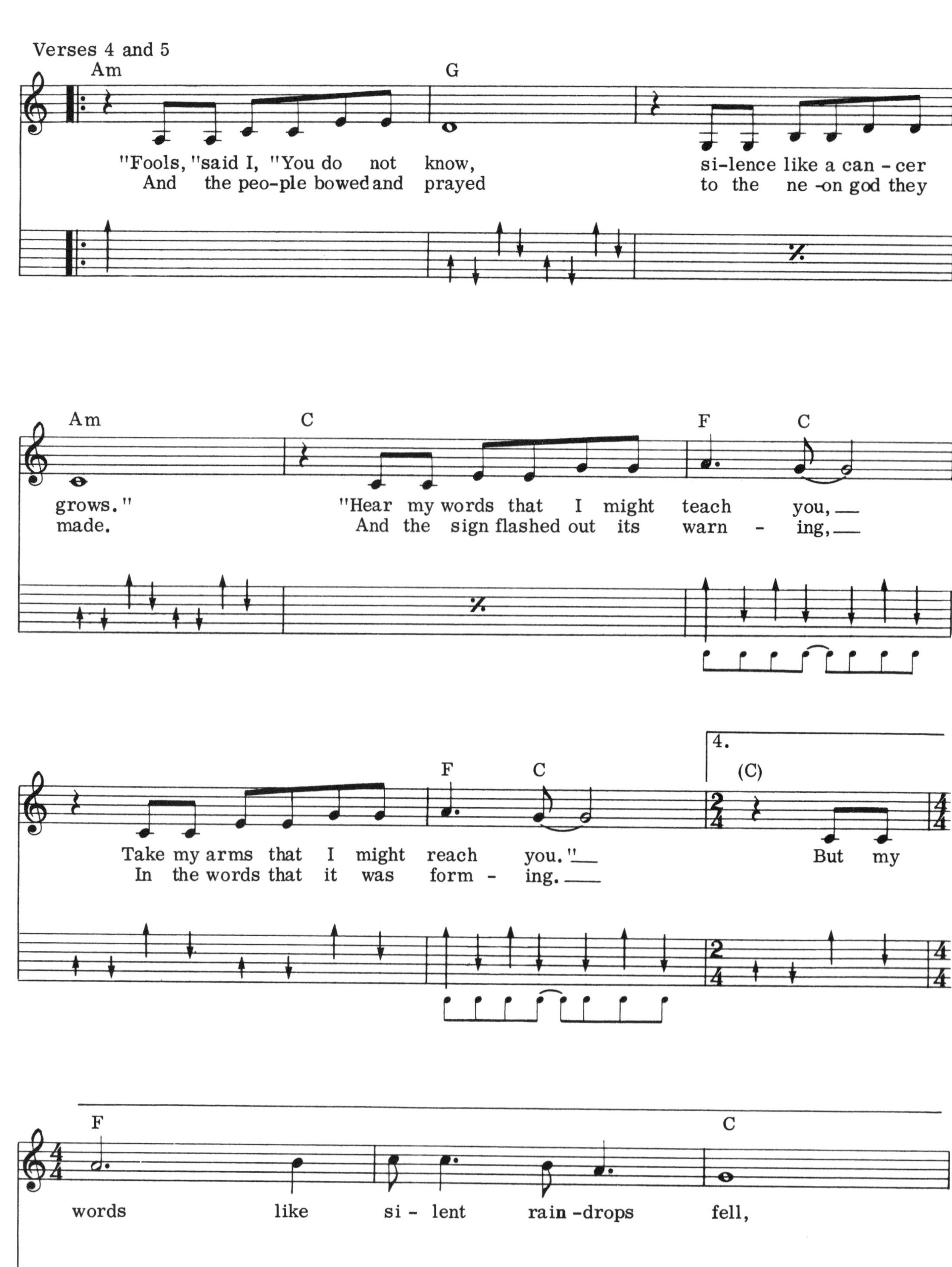
Verses 4 and 5
Am
G
"Fools," said I, "You do not know,
And the peo-ple bowed and prayed
si-lence like a can - cer
to the ne -on god they
Am
C
F
C
grows."
made.
"Hear my words that I might teach you, —
And the sign flashed out its warn - ing, —
4.
(C)
F
C
Take my arms that I might reach you." —
In the words that it was form - ing. —
But my
F
C
words like si - lent rain -drops fell,

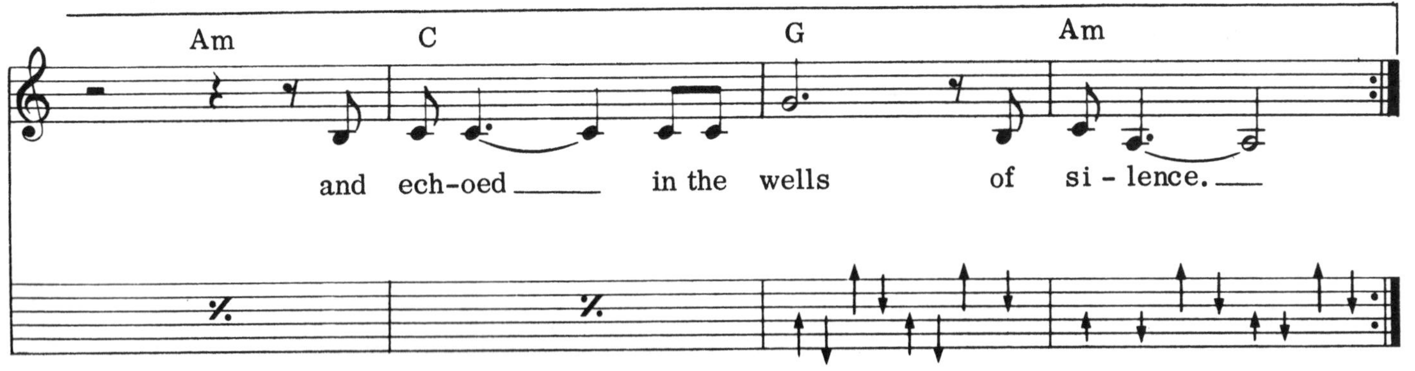

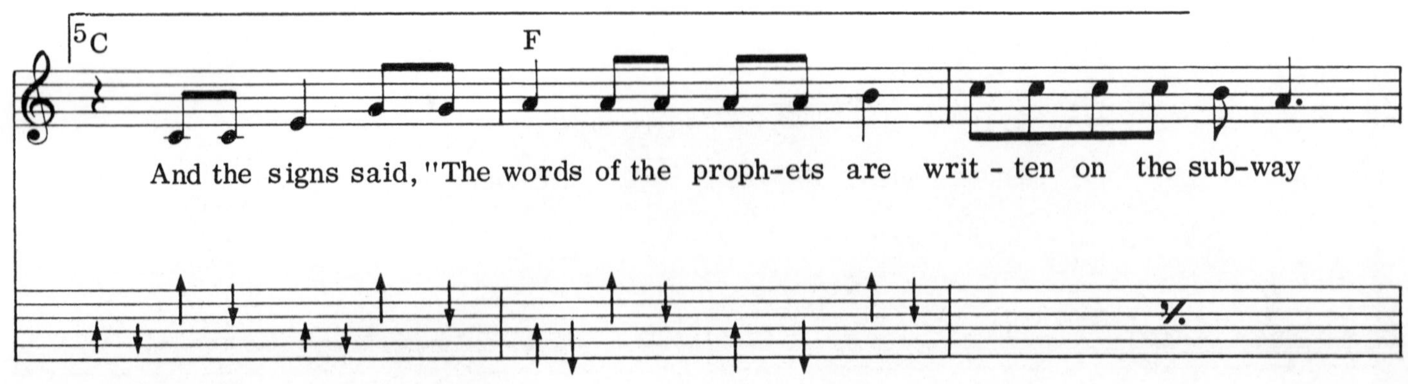

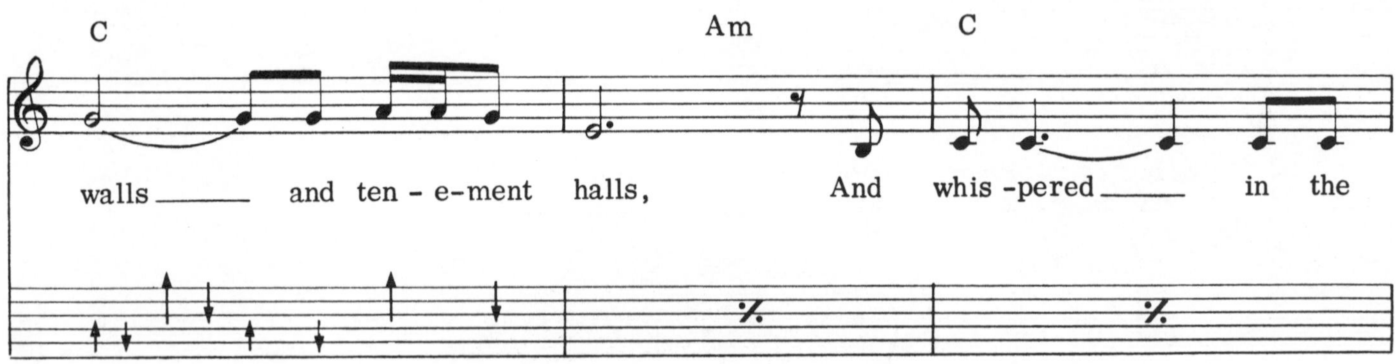

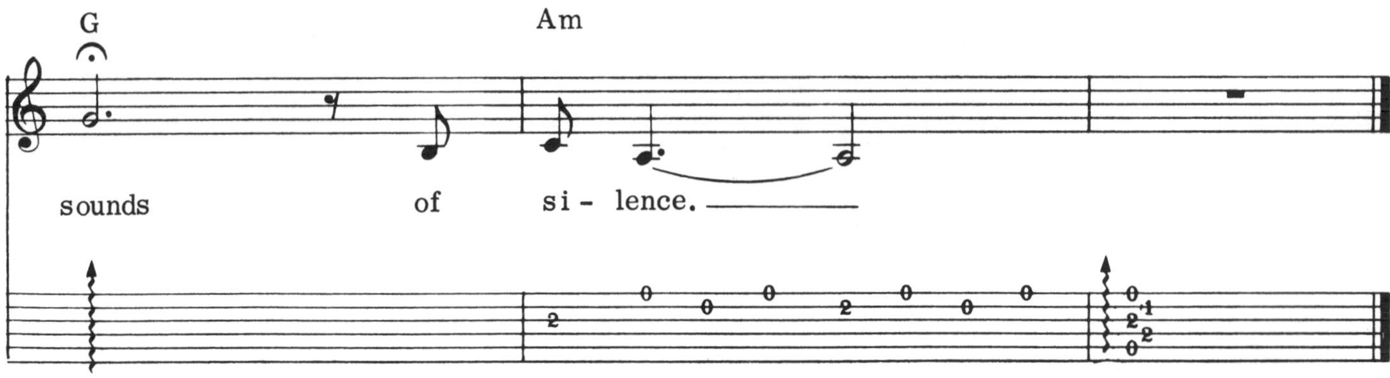

Fingerpicking as in 1st verse

I Am A Rock

For recorded key, Capo up 3 frets

Words and Music by
PAUL SIMON

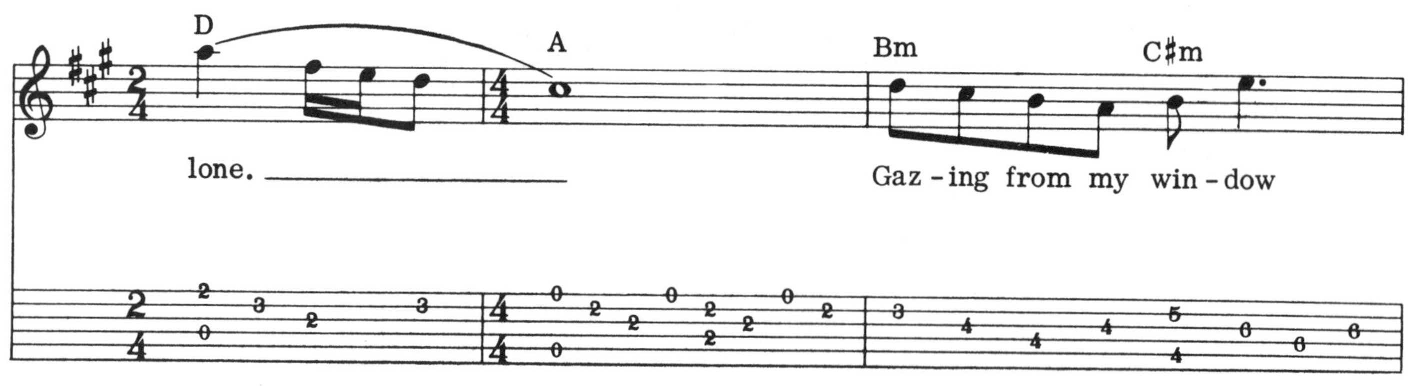
D
A
Bm
C♯m
lone.
Gaz - ing from my win - dow

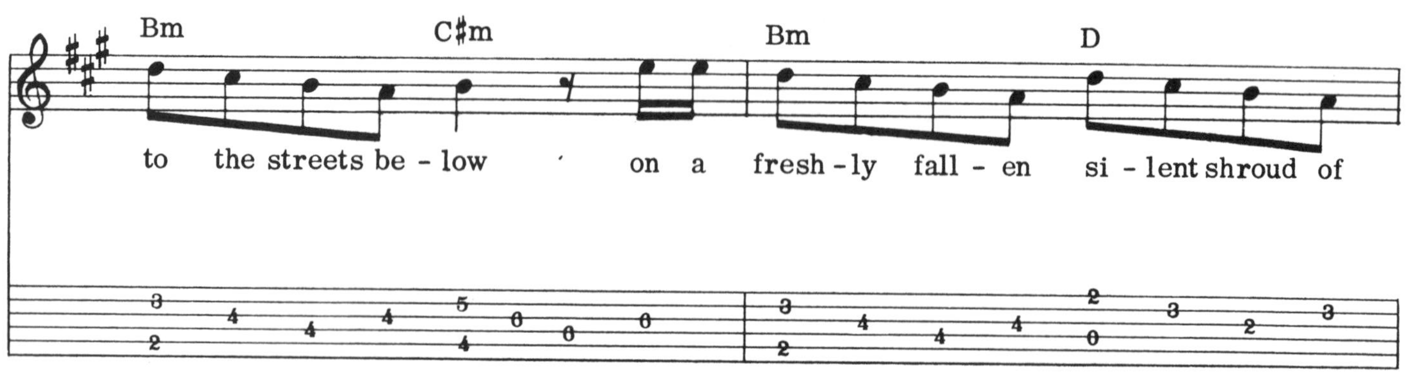
Bm
C♯m
Bm
D
to the streets be - low on a fresh - ly fall - en si - lent shroud of

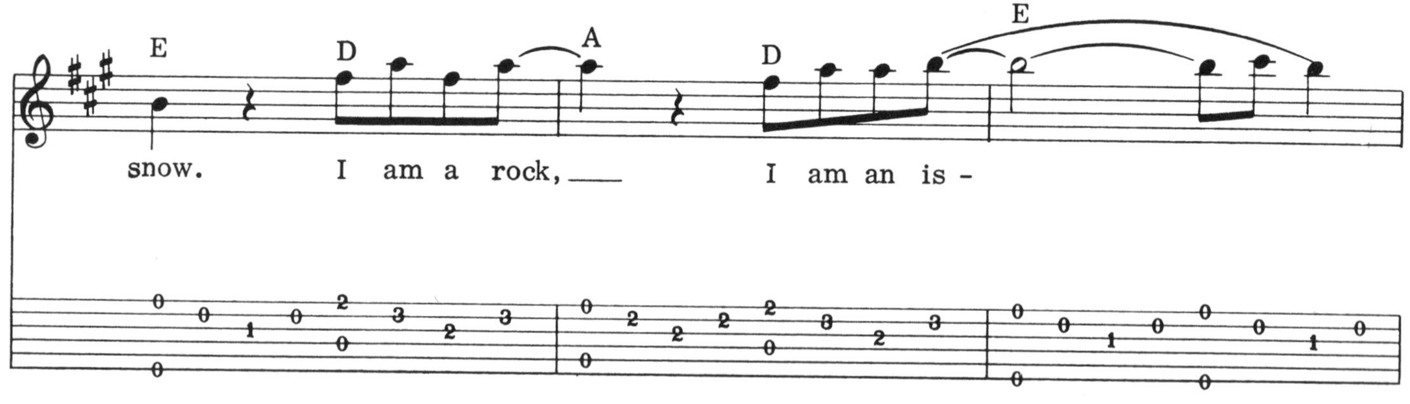
E
D
A
D
E
snow. I am a rock, I am an is -

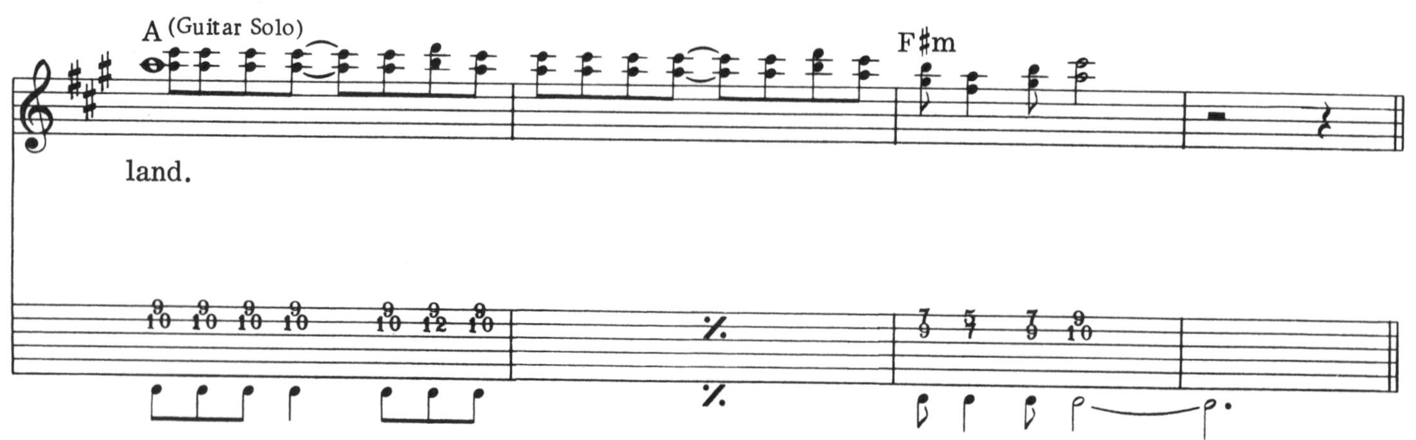
A (Guitar Solo)
F♯m
land.

Additional Words

A/ / / / / / / / D / / / A / / / / / / /
2. I've built walls a fortress deep and mighty,
Bm/ E / D / A / / /
That none may penetrate.
Bm / C♯m / Bm / C♯m /
I have no need of friendship, friendship causes pain.
Bm / D / E /
Its laughter and its loving I disdain.
D / A / D / E / / / A / / / / / / / F♯m / / / / / /
I am a rock, I am an is - land.

/ A / / / / / / / D / / / A / / / / / / /
3. Don't talk of love, I've heard the word before
Bm / E/ D / A / /
It's sleeping in my memory.
/ Bm / C♯m / Bm / C♯m
And I won't disturb the slumber of feelings that have died,
/ Bm / D / E /
If I never loved I never would have cried.
D / A / D / E / / / A / / / / / / / F♯m / / / / / /
I am a rock, I am an is - land.

/ A / / / / / / / D/ / / A / / / / / /
4. I have my books And my poetry to protect me.
/ Bm / E/ D / A / / /
I am shielded in my armour.
Bm / C♯m / Bm / C♯m /
Hiding in my room, Safe within my womb.
Bm / D E /
I touch no one and no one touches me.
D / A / D / E / / / A / / / / / /
I am a rock, I am an is - land.

Scarborough Fair/Canticle

For recorded key, Capo up 7 frets

Arrangement and Original
Counter Melody by
PAUL SIMON and
ART GARFUNKEL

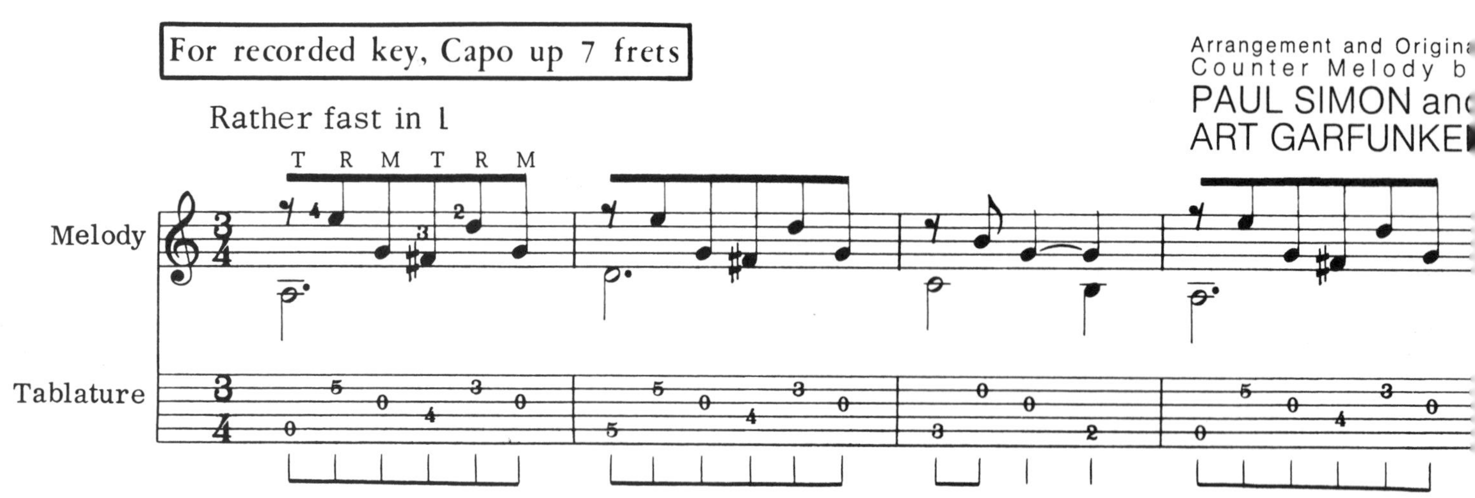

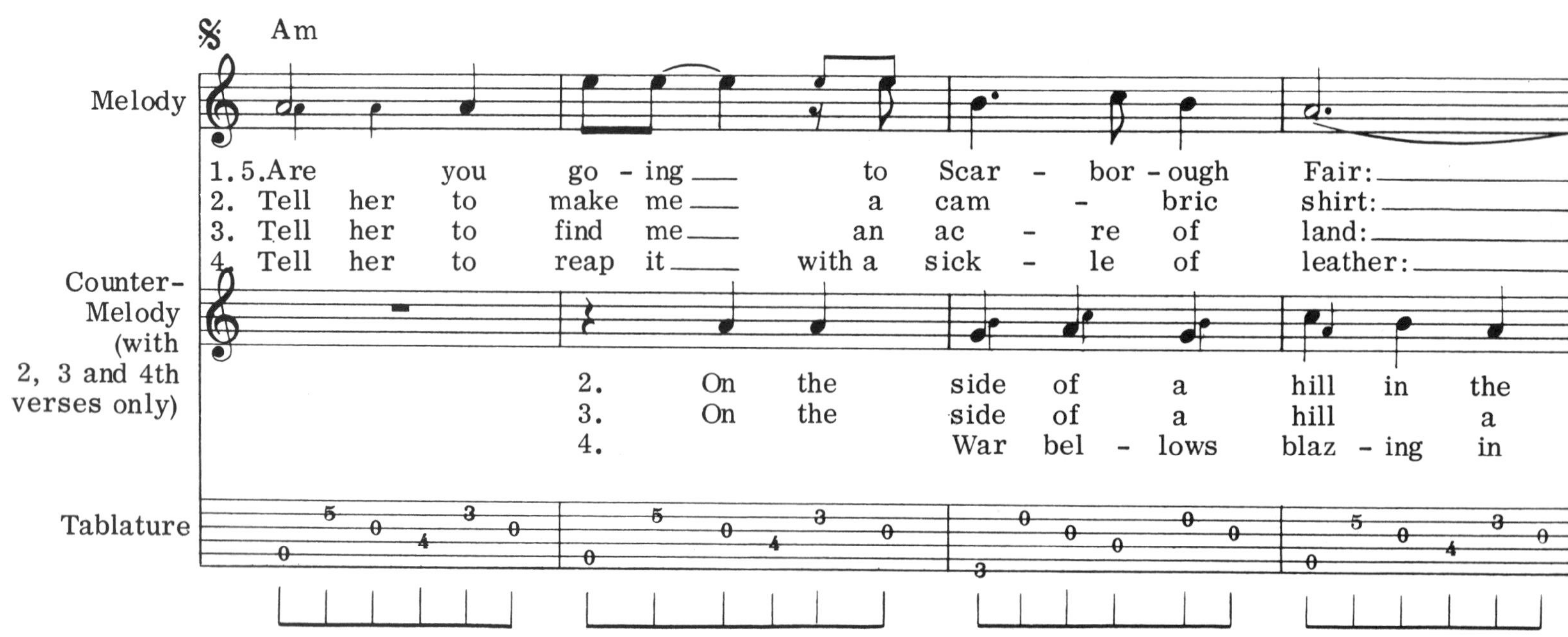

C
Am
C
D
Pars - ley, sage, rose - mar - y and
Pars - ley, sage, rose - mar - y and
Pars - ley, sage, rose - mar - y and
Pars - ley, sage, rose - mar - y and
deep for - est green
sprink - ling of leaves
scar - let bat - tal - ions
Am
thyme.
thyme.
thyme.
thyme.
Re -
With -
Be -
And
Trac - ing of spar - row on snow - crest - ed brown.
Wash - es the grave with sil - ver - y tears.
Gen - er - als or - der their sol - diers to kill.
C
(Bm)
(Am)
G
mem - ber me to one who lives there
out no seams nor nee - dle work
tween the salt wa - ter and the sea strands,
gather it all in a bunch of heather,
Blan - kets and bed - clothes the
A sol - dier cleans and
And to fight for a cause they've

last time
to Coda
Am
G
(Am)
(G)
(Am)
(G)
She was once a true love of
Then she'll be a true love of
Then she'll be a true love of
Then she'll be a true love of
child of the moun - tain
pol - ishes a gun.
long a - go for - got - ten.
D.S. for verses 2,3,4,5
last time skip to Coda
Am
mine.
mine.
mine.
mine.
Sleeps un - a - ware of the clar - i - on call.
Coda
Am
mine.

Homeward Bound

For recorded key, Capo up 4 frets

Words and Music by
PAUL SIMON

po - et and a one - man band.
minds me that I long to be
need some - one to com - fort me.
Home - ward
C
G
C
Bound, I wish I was, Home - ward Bound.
Full strokes of the open R.H.
G
Bass run
G
Bass run
Home, where my thought's es - cap - ing, Home, where my mu - sic's play - ing,
G
Bass run
D7
Home, where my love lies wait - ing si - lent - ly
G
Play 3 times
C
G
for me.
2.
3. To -

Bridge Over Troubled Water

Words and Music by
PAUL SIMON

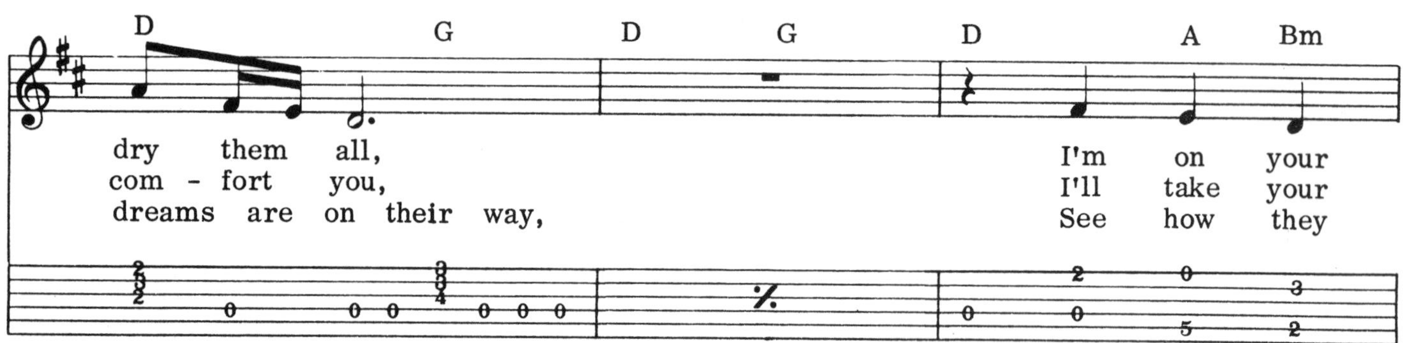
D
G
D
G
D
A
Bm
dry them all, I'm on your
com - fort you, I'll take your
dreams are on their way, See how they

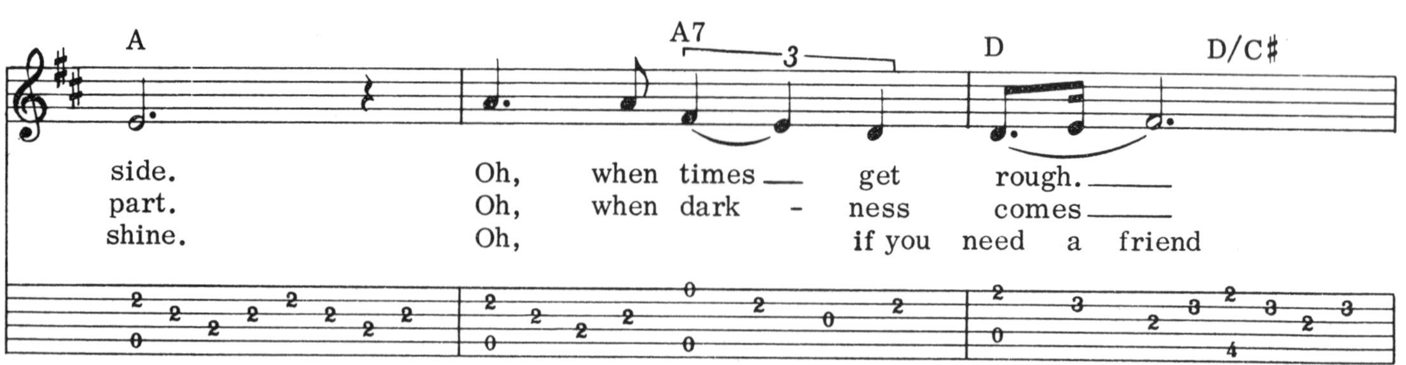
A
A7
3
D
D/C♯
side. Oh, when times get rough.
part. Oh, when dark - ness comes
shine. Oh, if you need a friend

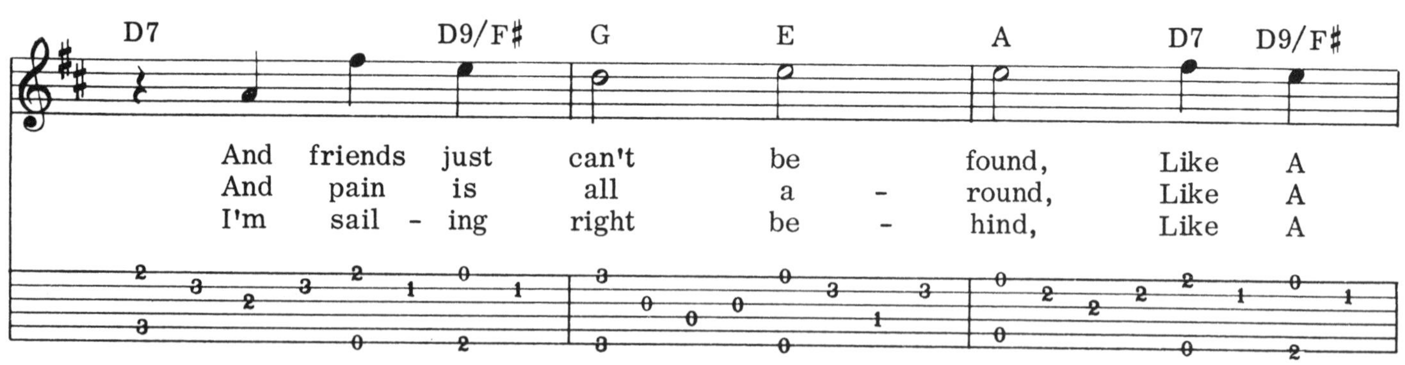
D7
D9/F♯
G
E
A
D7
D9/F♯
And friends just can't be found, Like A
And pain is all a - round, Like A
I'm sail - ing right be - hind, Like A

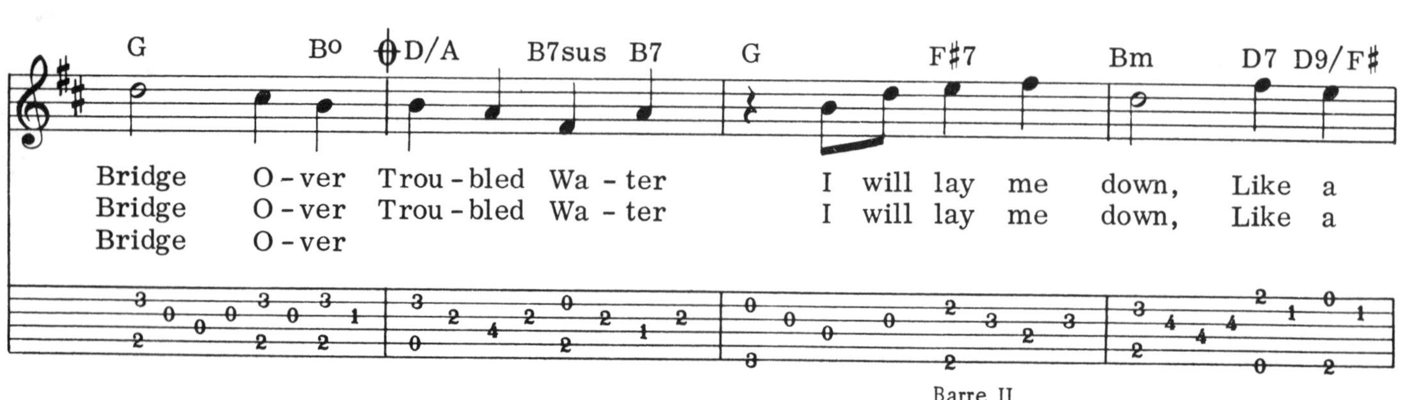
G
Bo
D/A
B7sus
B7
G
F♯7
Bm
D7
D9/F♯
Bridge O - ver Trou - bled Wa - ter I will lay me down, Like a
Bridge O - ver Trou - bled Wa - ter I will lay me down, Like a
Bridge O - ver
Barre II

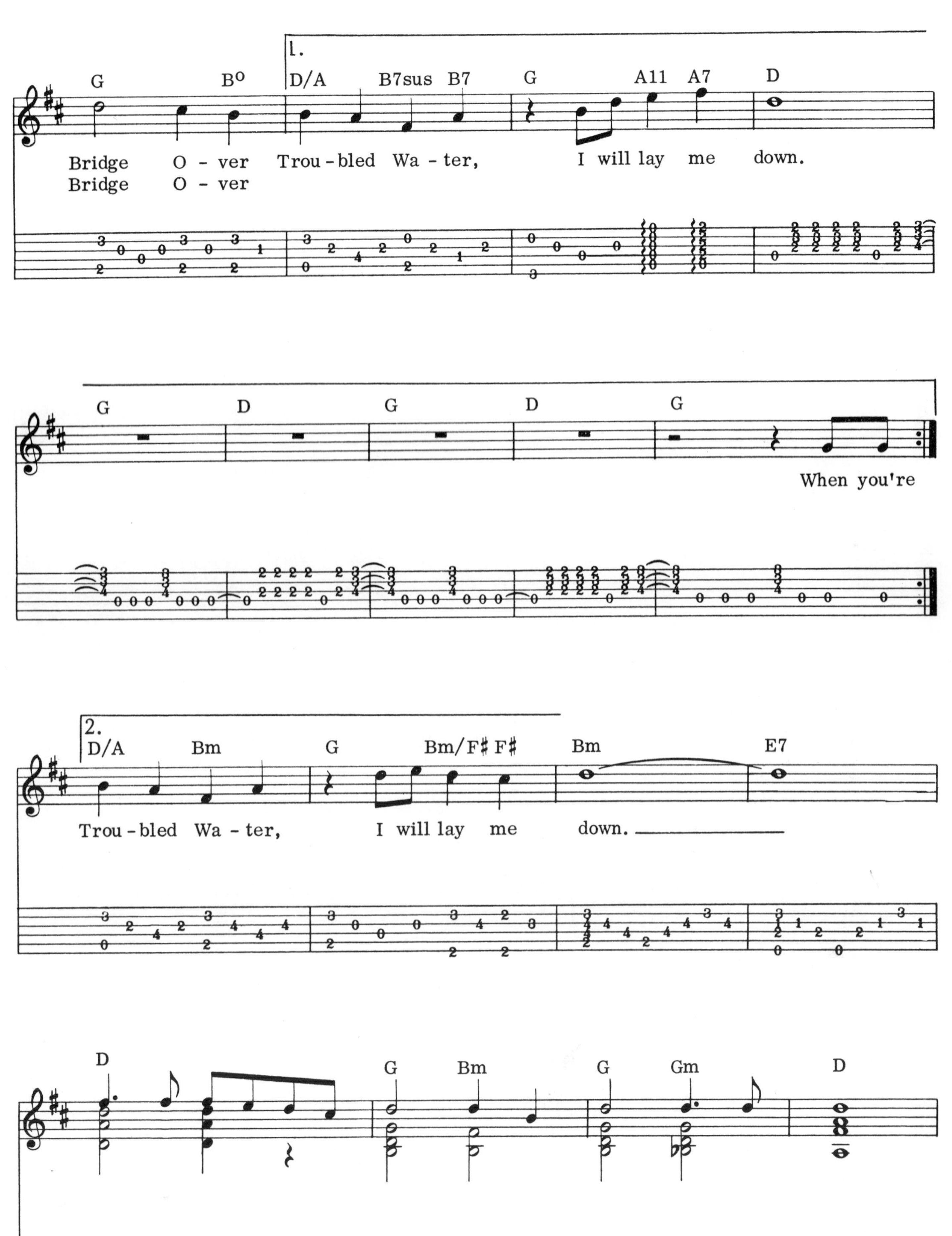
1.
G
B°
D/A
B7sus
B7
G
A11
A7
D
Bridge O - ver Trou - bled Wa - ter, I will lay me down.
Bridge O - ver
G
D
G
D
G
When you're
2.
D/A
Bm
G
Bm/F♯ F♯
Bm
E7
Trou - bled Wa - ter, I will lay me down.
D
G
Bm
G
Gm
D

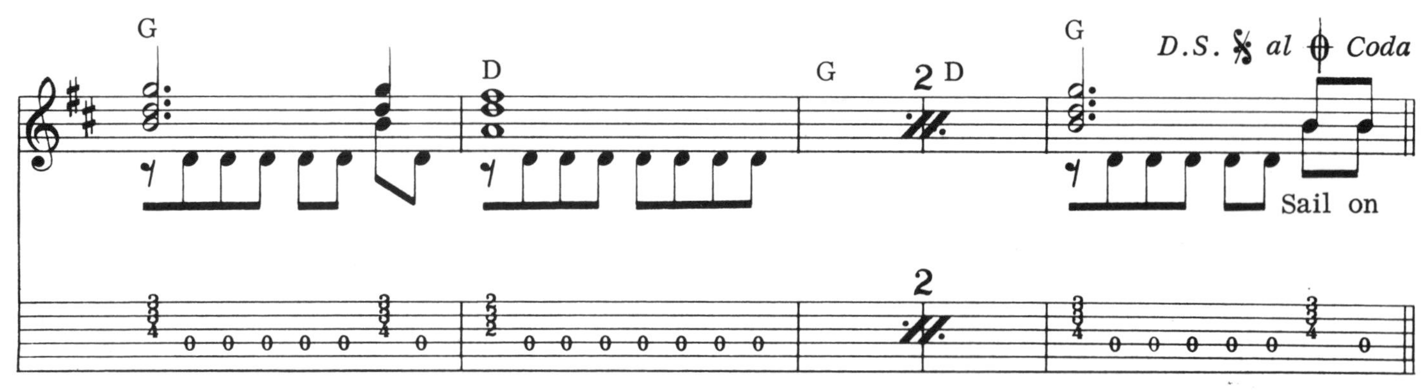
G
D
G
2 D
G
D.S. al Coda
Sail on
2

Coda
D/A
Bm
G
Bm/F♯ F♯
Bm
D7 D9/F♯
G
E7
Trou-bled Wa-ter, I will ease your mind, Like a Bridge O-ver

D/A
Bm
G
F♯7
Bm
E7
Trou-bled Wa-ter, I will ease your mind.

D/A
G
Gm
D

August 1968

America

For recorded key, Capo up 2 frets

Words and Music by
PAUL SIMON

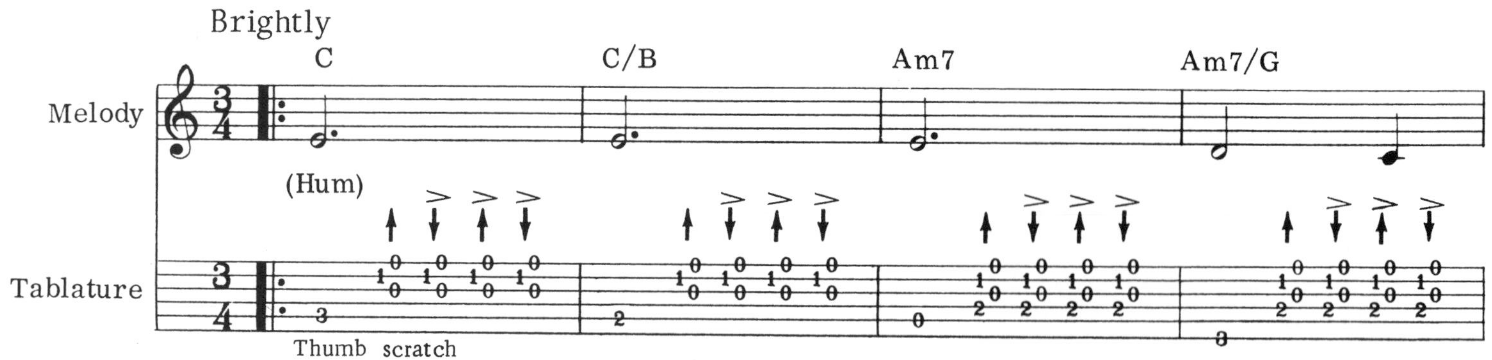

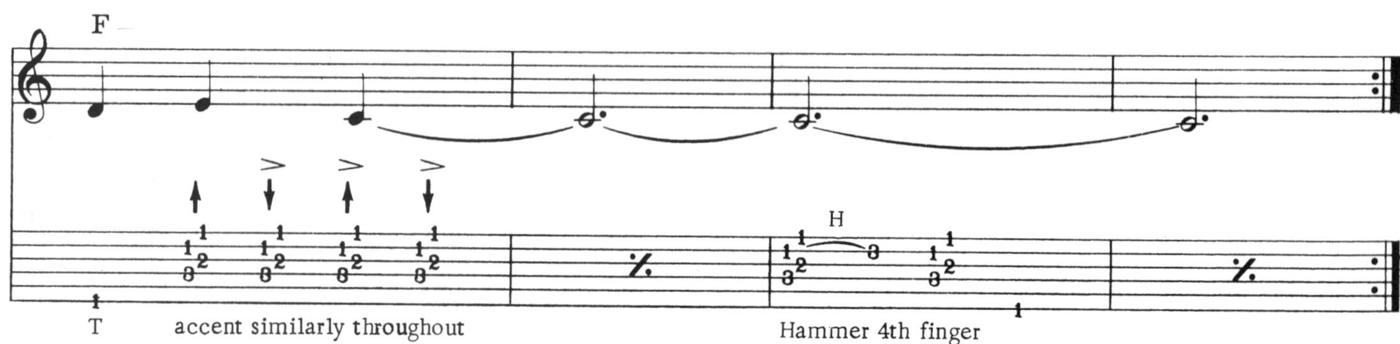

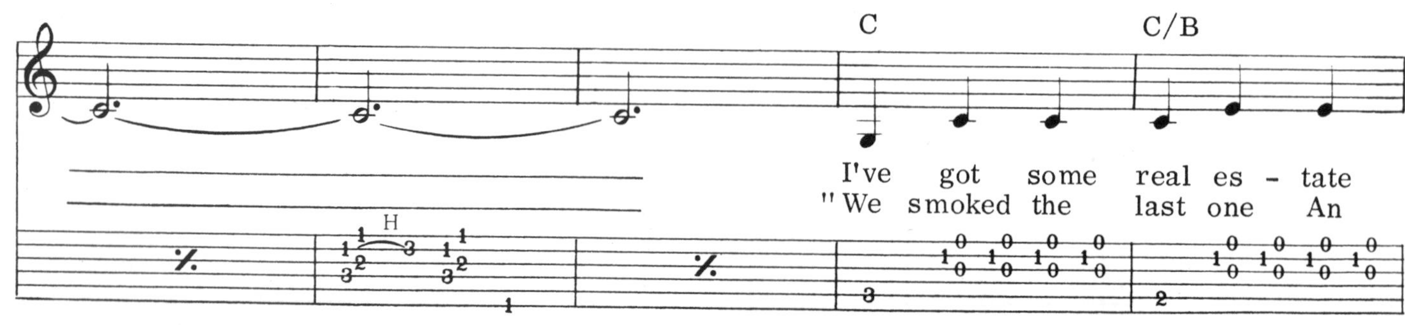

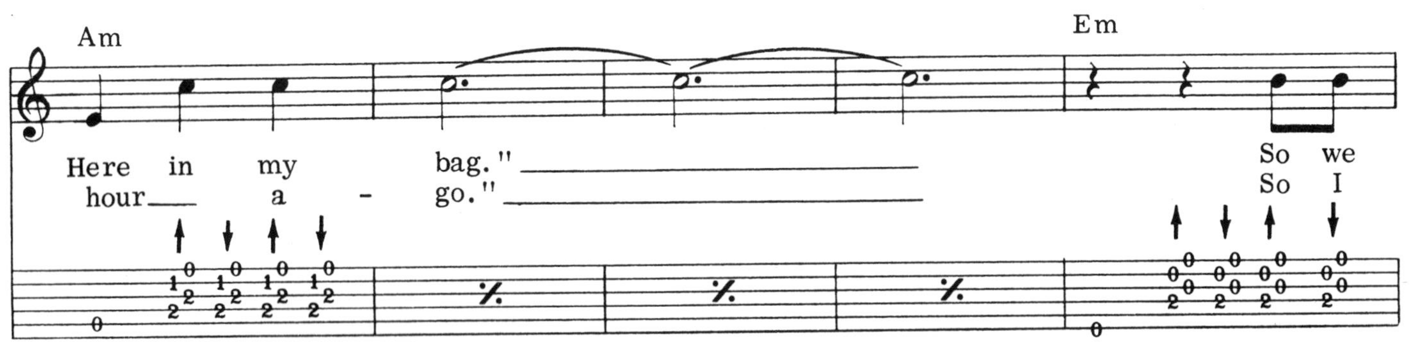
Am
Em
Here in my bag." So we
hour a - go." So I

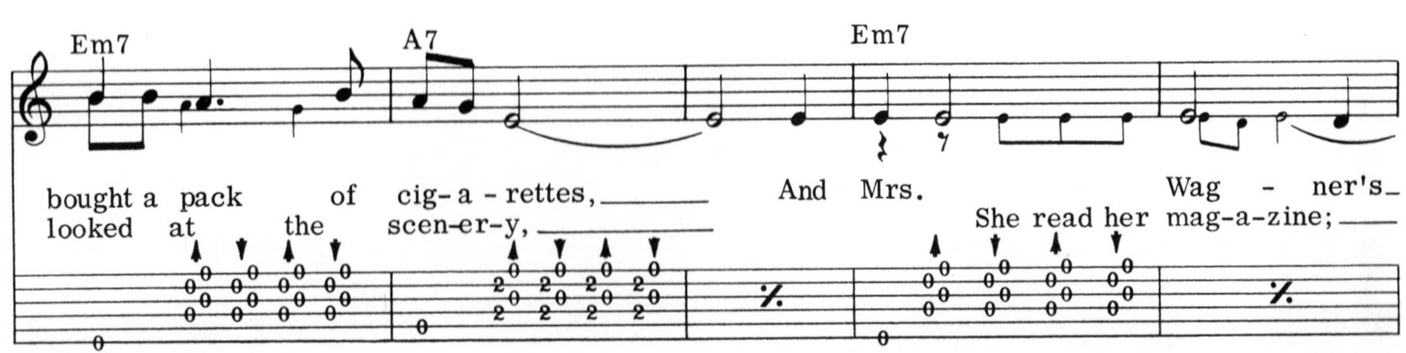
Em7
A7
Em7
bought a pack of cig-a-rettes, And Mrs. Wag - ner's
looked at the scen-er-y, She read her mag-a-zine;

A7
D
C
G
pies, And walked off to look for A -
And the moon rose o - ver an
Sim.

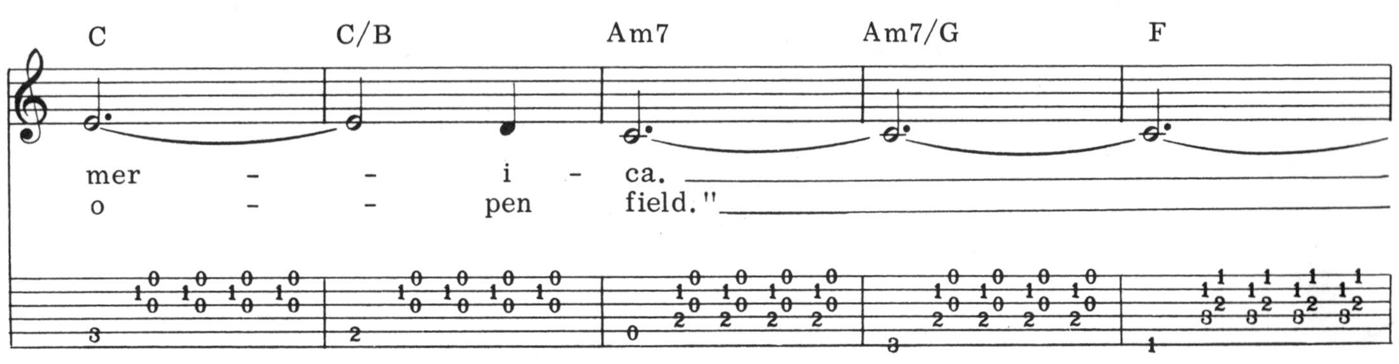
C
C/B
Am7
Am7/G
F
mer - - i - ca.
o - - pen field."

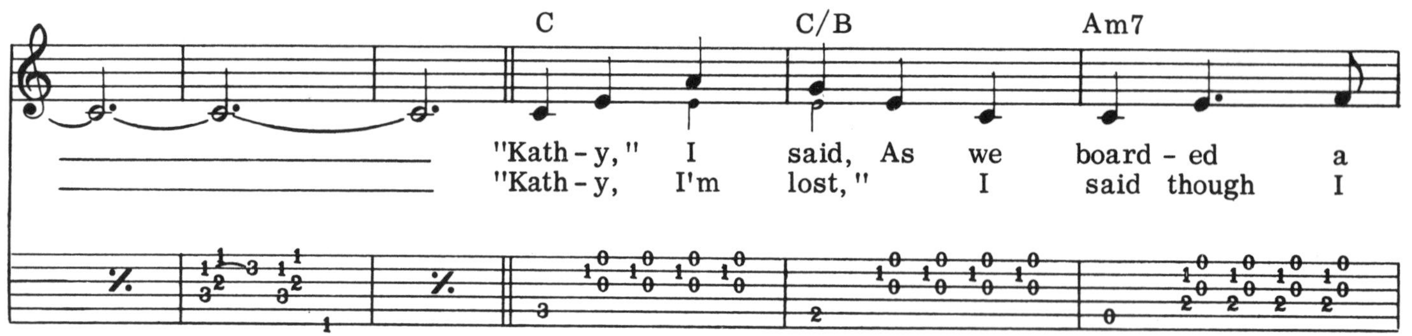
C
C/B
Am7
"Kath - y," I said, As we board - ed a
"Kath - y, I'm lost," I said though I

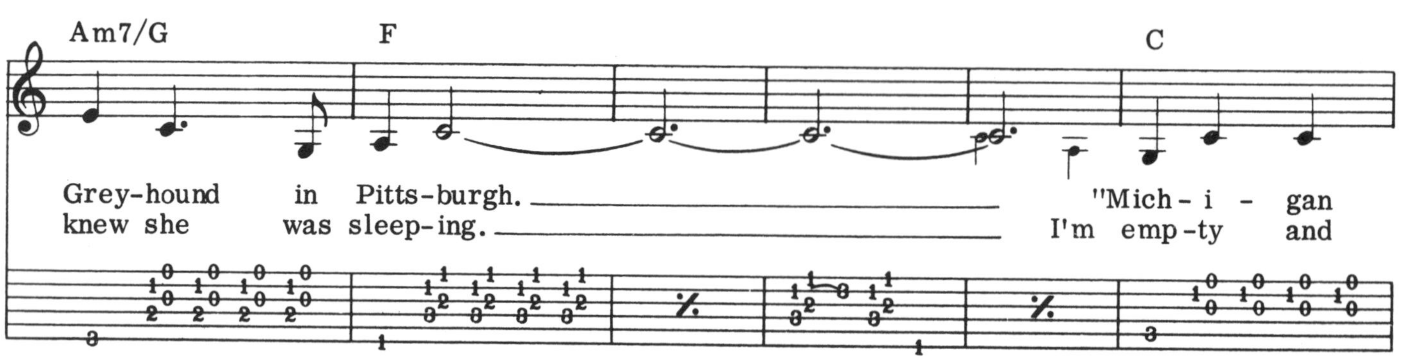
Am7/G
F
C
Grey-hound in Pitts-burgh.
knew she was sleep-ing.
"Mich - i - gan
I'm emp -ty and

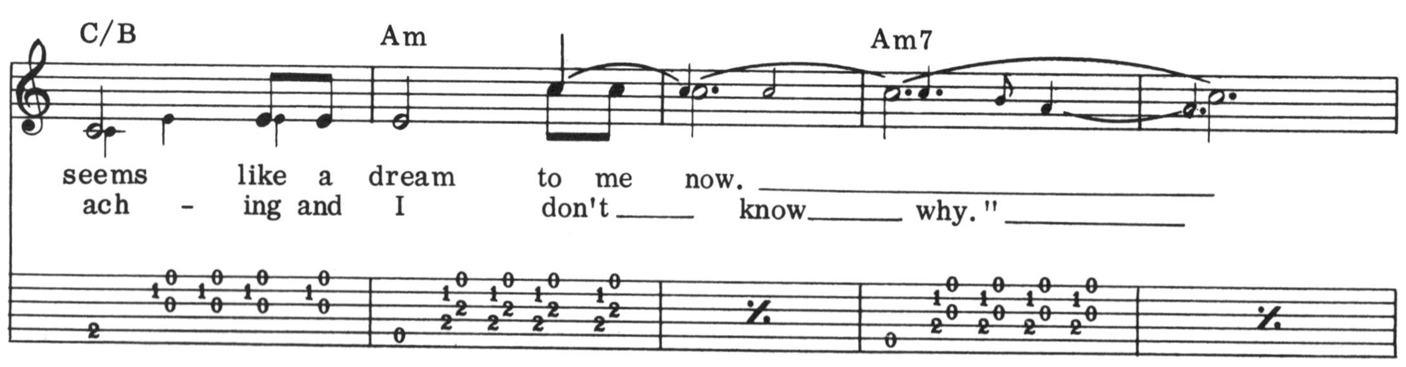
C/B
Am
Am7
seems like a dream to me now.
ach - ing and I don't know why."

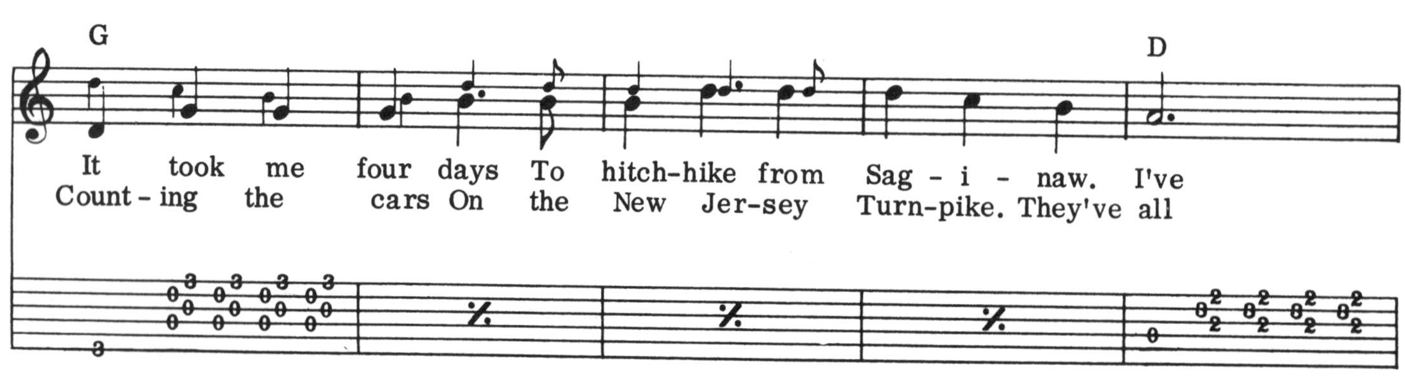
G
D
It took me four days To hitch-hike from Sag - i - naw. I've
Count - ing the cars On the New Jer-sey Turn-pike. They've all

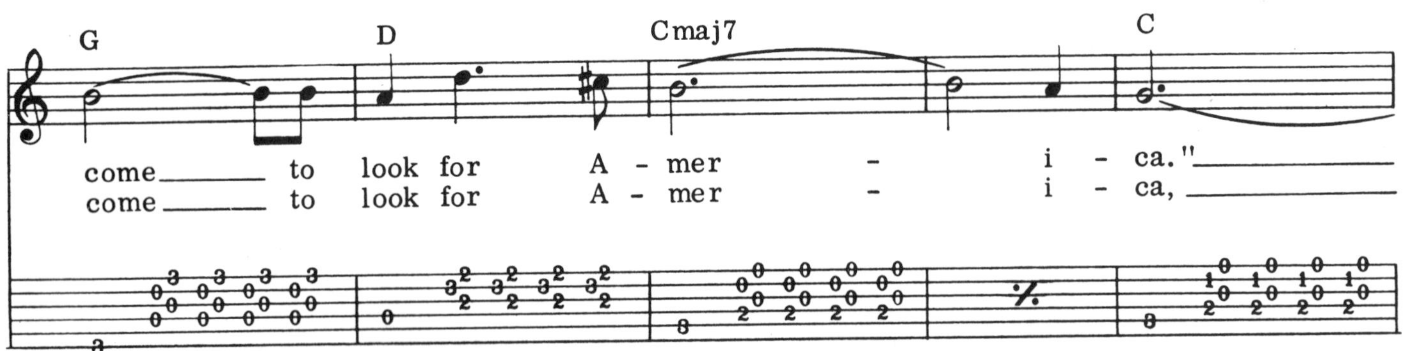
G
D
Cmaj7
C
come to look for A - mer - i - ca."
come to look for A - mer - i - ca,

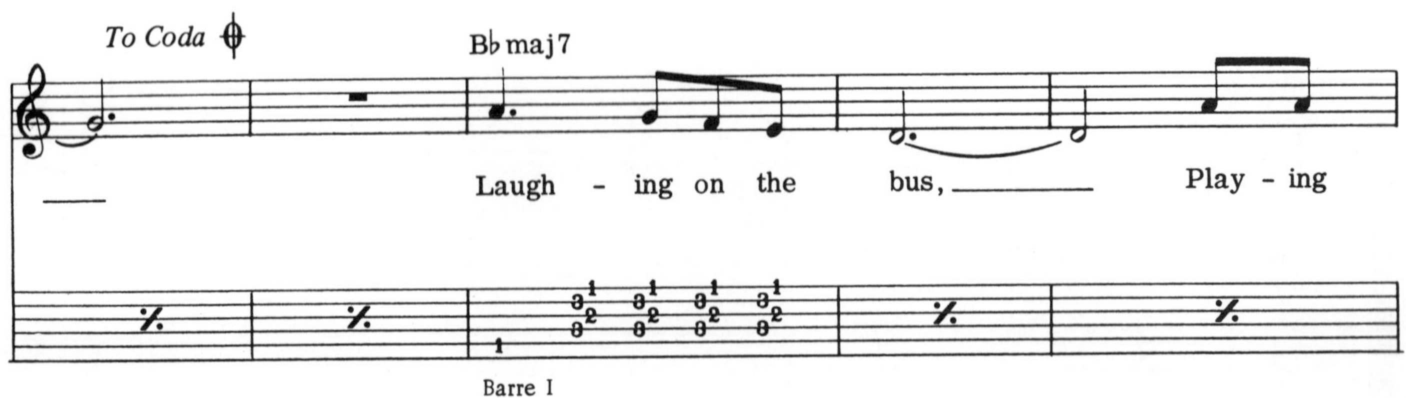
To Coda
B♭maj7
Laugh - ing on the bus, Play - ing
Barre I

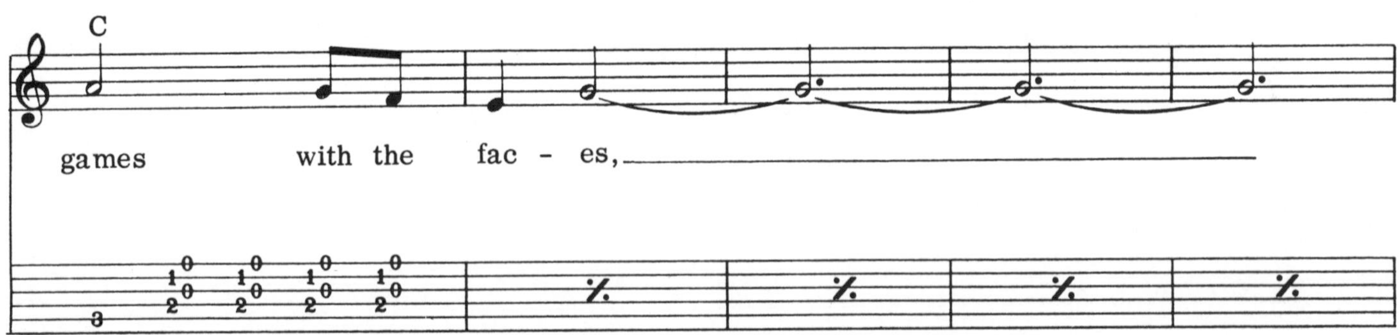
C
games with the fac - es,

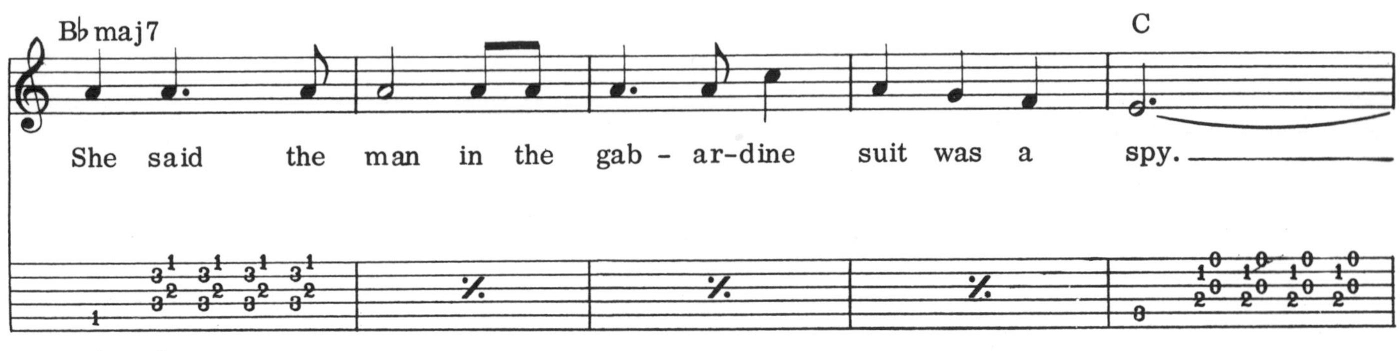
B♭maj7
C
She said the man in the gab - ar-dine suit was a spy.
Barre I

F
I said, "Be care - ful, His
Fmaj7
C
C/G
bow - tie is real - ly a cam - 'ra."
Am/F♯
Fmaj7
D.S. al Coda
Coda
D
G
D
All come to look for A -
Cmaj7
C
Repeat and fade
mer - i - ca.

Kathy's Song

No Capo required

Words and Music by
PAUL SIMON

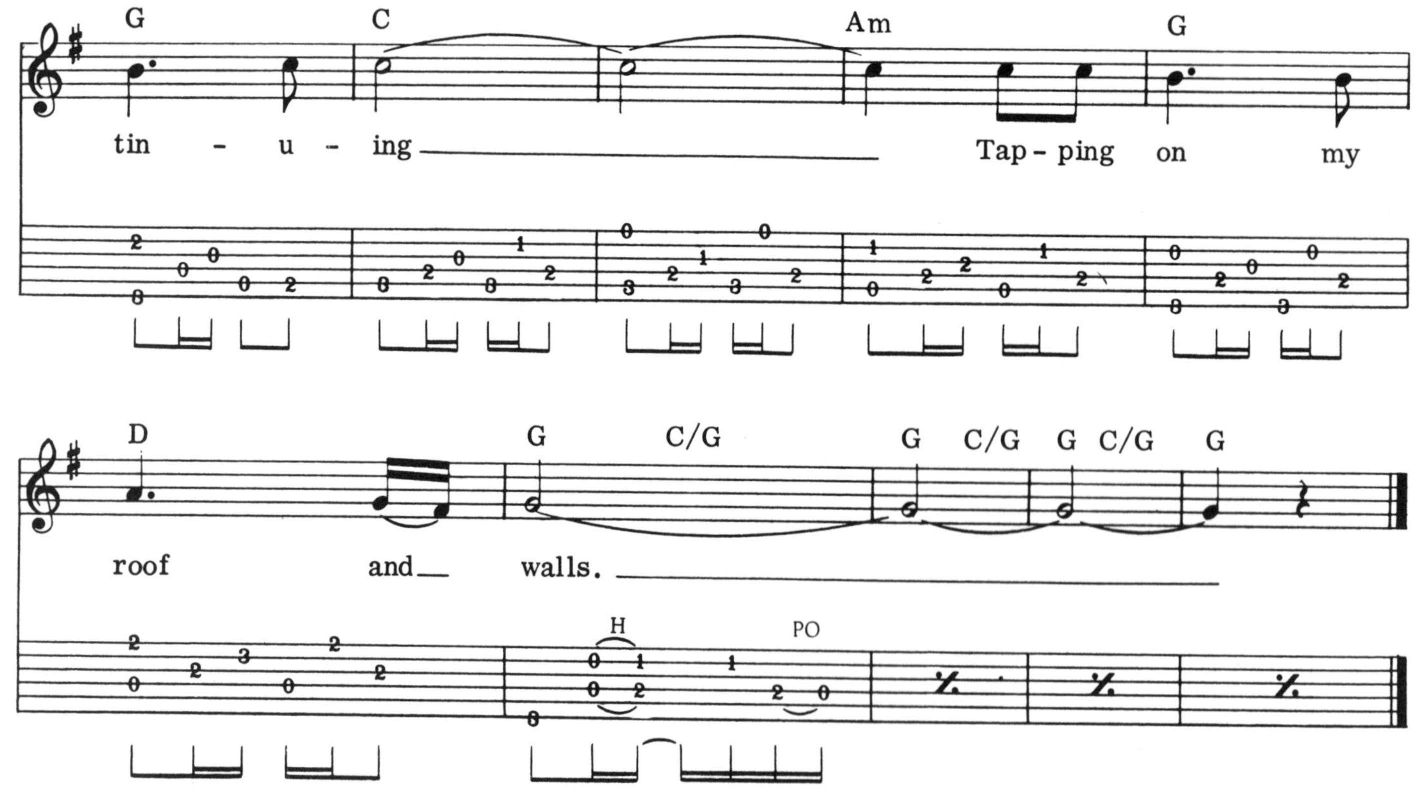

Additional Words

2. And from the shelter of my mind
Through the window of my eyes
I gaze beyond the rain-drenched streets
To England where my heart lies.

3. My mind's distracted and diffused
My thoughts are many miles away
They lie with you when you're asleep
And kiss you when you start your day.

4. And a song I was writing is left undone
I don't know why I spend my time
Writing songs I can't believe
With words that tear and strain to rhyme.

5. And so you see I have come to doubt
All that I once held as true
I stand alone without beliefs
The only truth I know is you.

6. And as I watch the drops of rain
Weave their weary paths and die
I know that I am like the rain
There but for the grace of you go I.

El Condor Pasa

English Lyric by
PAUL SIMON
Musical Arrangement by
J. MILCHBERG AND D. ROBLES

C
G
way, I'd rath - er sail a - way Like a swan that's here and
C
gone. A man gets tied up to the ground, He gives the
G
Em
world its sad-dest sound, its sad-dest sound.
G
I'd rath-er be a for-est than a street. Yes, I
Em
would, if I could, I surely would. I'd

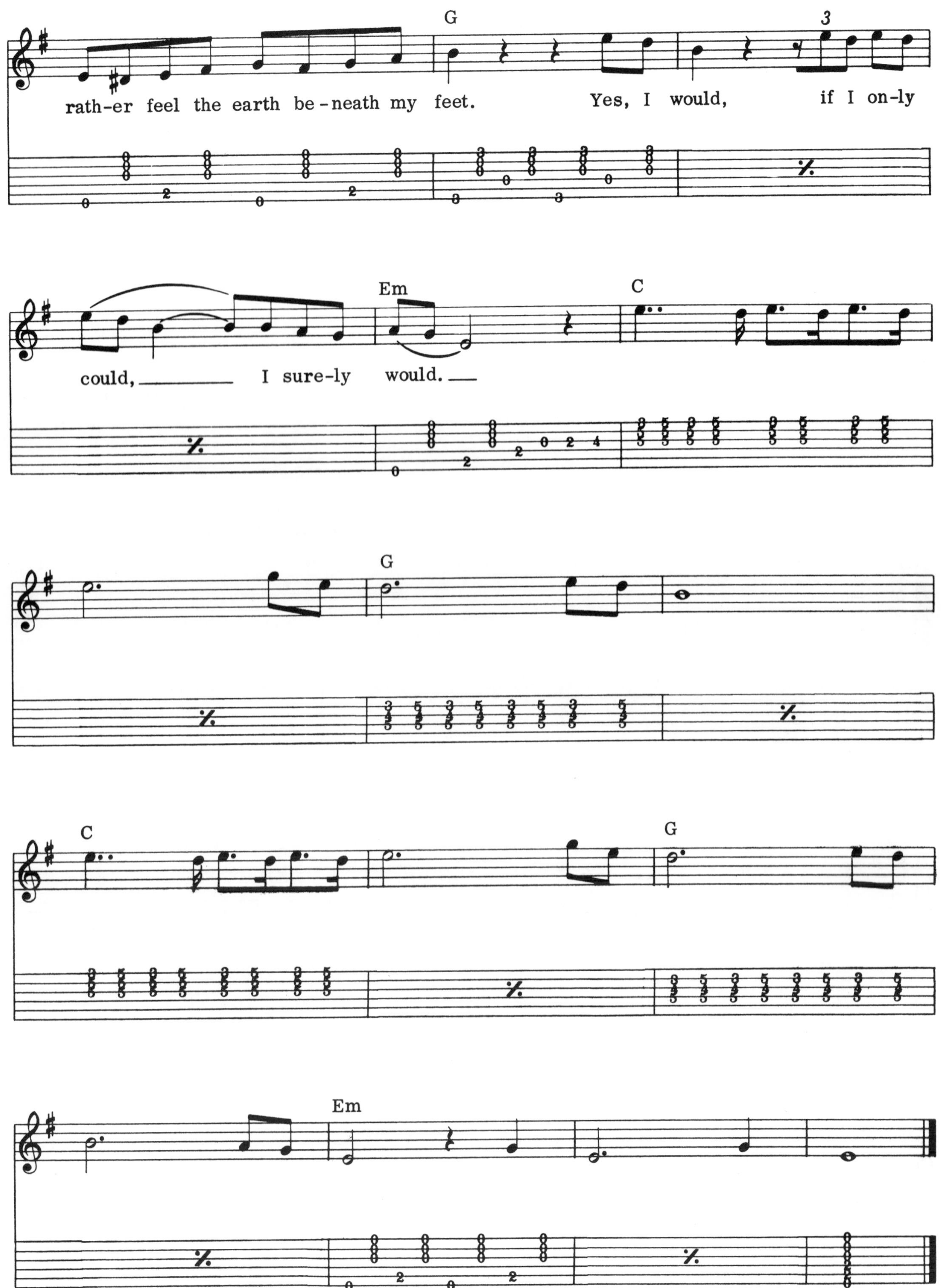
G
3
rath-er feel the earth be-neath my feet. Yes, I would, if I on-ly
Em
C
could, I sure-ly would.
G
C
G
Em

Bookends

No Capo required

Words and Music by
PAUL SIMON

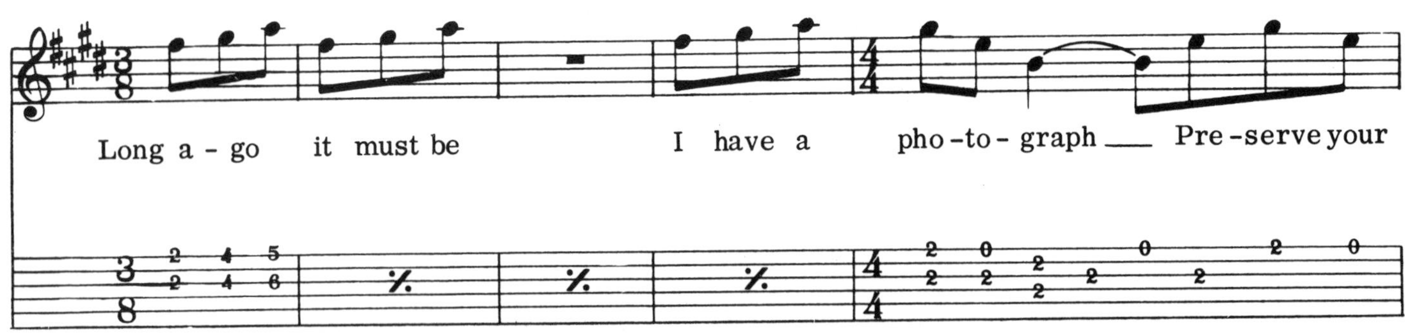
Long a - go it must be I have a pho-to-graph Pre-serve your

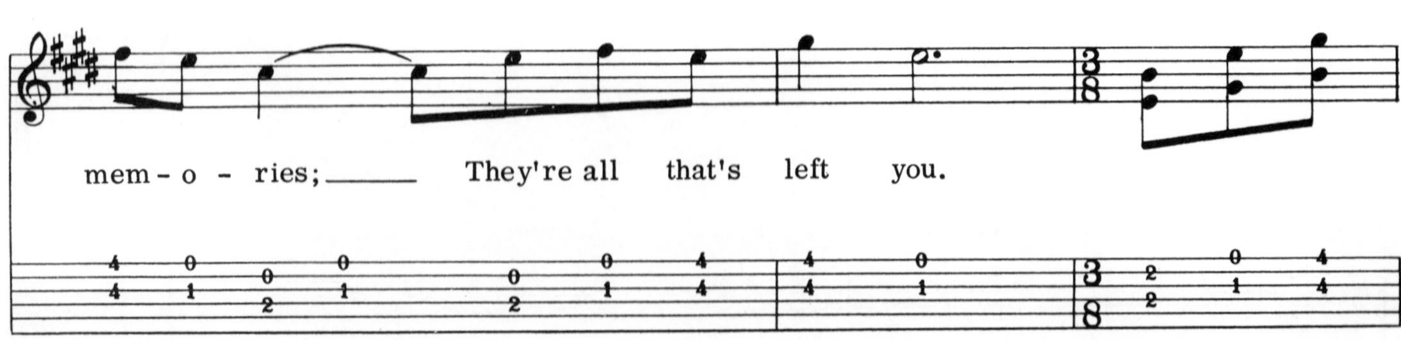
mem - o - ries; They're all that's left you.

H/PO

Cecilia

Words and Music by
PAUL SIMON

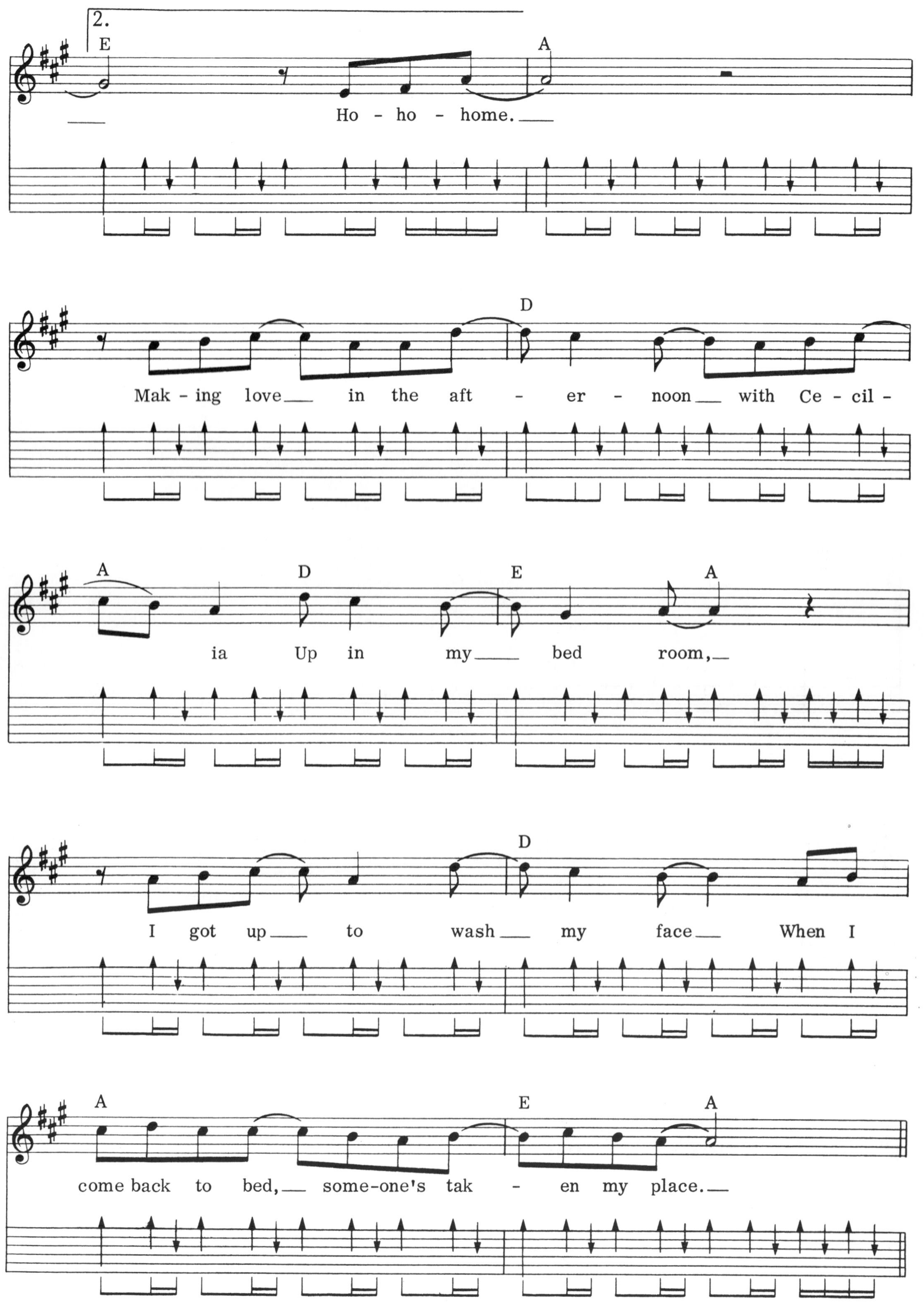
2.
E
A
Ho - ho - home.
D
Mak - ing love in the aft - er - noon with Ce - cil -
A
D
E
A
ia Up in my bed room,
D
I got up to wash my face When I
A
E
A
come back to bed, some-one's tak - en my place.

Additional Words

A/ / /   D   /   A /
Cel-ia,   you're breaking my heart,
        D   /   D   /   E / /
You're shaking my confidence dai-ly.
 /   D / A /   D   /   A /
Oh, Ce-cil - ia, I'm down on my knees,
    D   /   A   /   E / /
I'm begging you please to come home,
       / A //
Come on home.
 /   /   /   /   /   D   /   /   /   E   / /
Poh poh poh poh poh poh poh poh poh poh poh poh poh.
  / D / A /   D   /   A /
Jubi-la - tion, She loves me again
  D   /   A   / E   / /
I fall on the floor   and I laugh-ing.
  / D / A   /   D   /   A /
Jubi-la - tion,   She loves me   again
  D   /   A   / E   / /
I fall on the floor   and I laugh-ing.
 / D / A /
Oh, oh oh, oh
   D   /   A /
Oh oh oh oh oh
   D   /   A   E   //
Oh oh oh oh oh   oh oh oh   oh
 / D / A /
Oh oh oh oh
   D   /   A /
Oh oh oh oh oh
   D   /   A   /   E   //
Oh oh oh oh oh   oh oh oh   oh
       / A /// ///
Come on home.

Printed by Printwise (Haverhill) Limited, Suffolk

2/11 (177289)